I Am Me

Yasumasa Yonehara

Pocko Editions
London

Published by Pocko Editions

Design by Olga Norman
Text by Marc Hulson
Cover text by Lucien Rothenstein
Translation by Takako Kinoshita
and Machi Sugimoto
Printed in Italy by Grafiche Milani

ISBN 1-903977-07-X

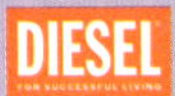

I Am Me

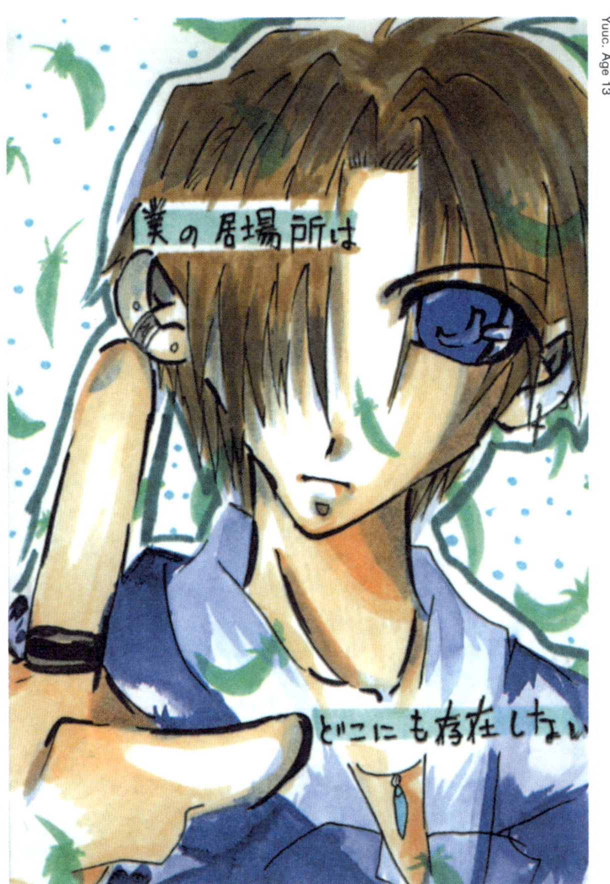

Yuuc. Age 13

There is no place for me.

Asahi. Age 14

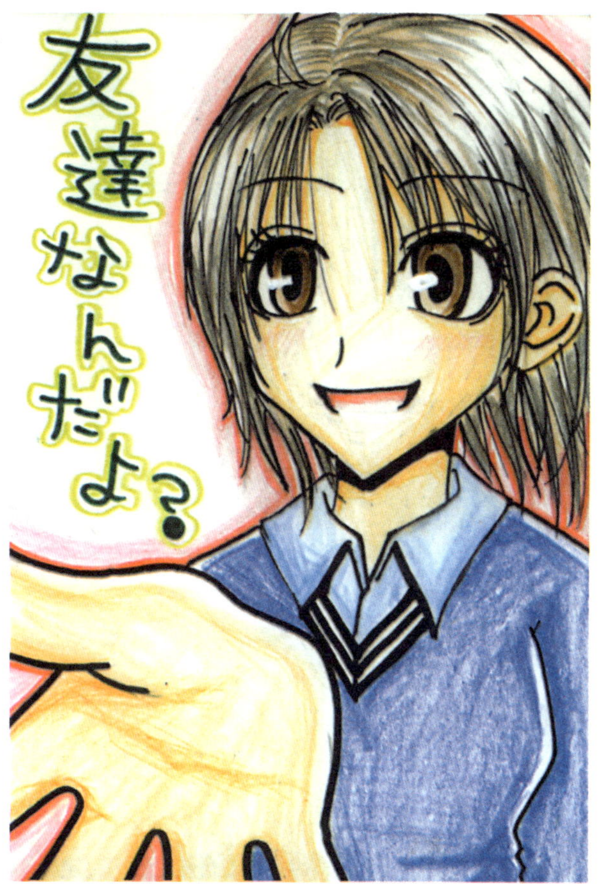

Aren't we friends?

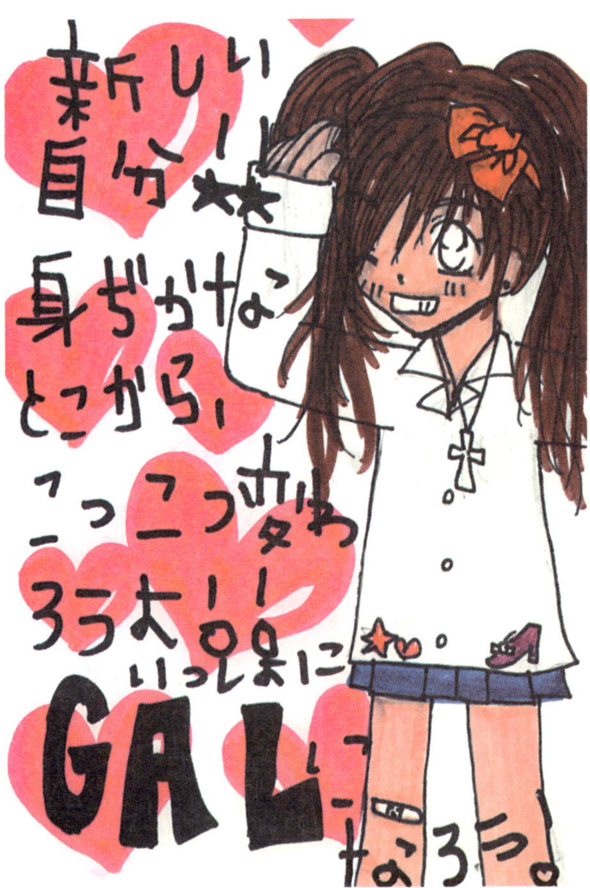

Ani wa Masaki. Age 13

Renew yourself!! Start making things change close to you. Let's become GAL with me.

Mamikko. Age 12

もっとキレイに
なってやる!!

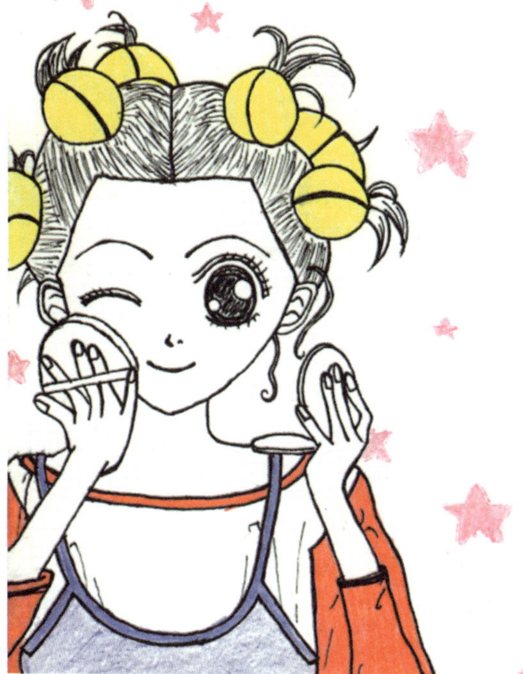

I will be more beautiful.

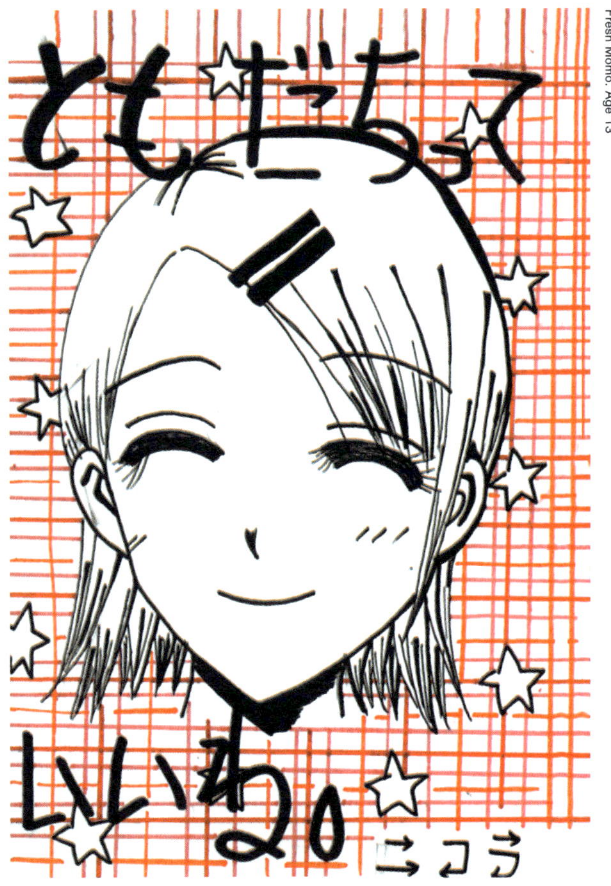

Fresh Momo. Age 13

It's nice being a friend with you.

Nana. Age 14

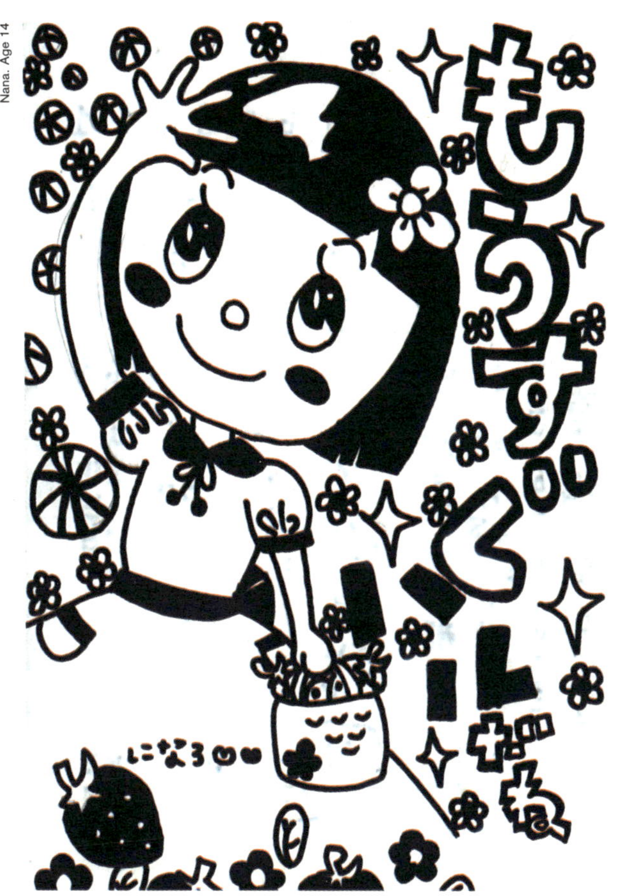

Spring is coming soon.

Yuuki. Age 13

初とうこう!!

泣きたいトキもある。

笑いたいトキもある。

それが今のあなただから。

あしたに向かって走れ!!

あたしは、あたし。

あなたはあなた。

Bye Bye

by ゆうき

You sometimes want to cry, sometimes want to smile, don't you?
That is you. Run toward tomorrow!! I am me, and you are you.

Risa Takahashi. Age 14

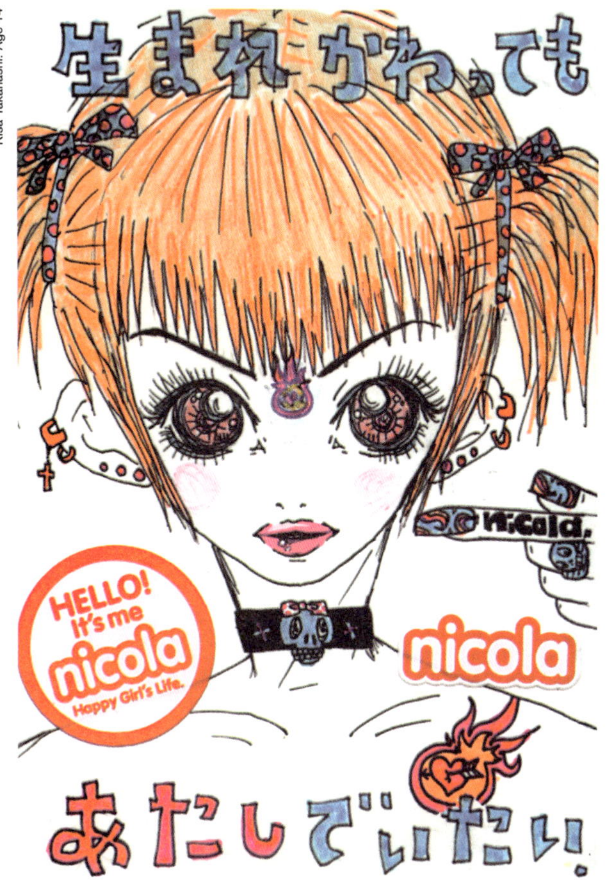

I wanna be me even in the next life.

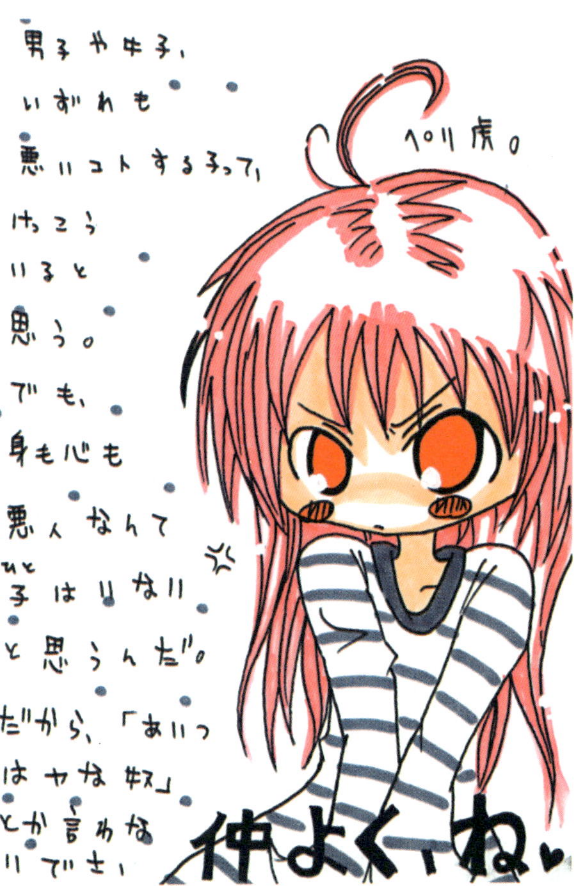

Peritora. Age 12

Both boys and girls are nasty sometimes. But there is no one who is a true evil, I believe. So don't tell me "I hate him", Be nice to eachother.

Omana Mana. Age 13

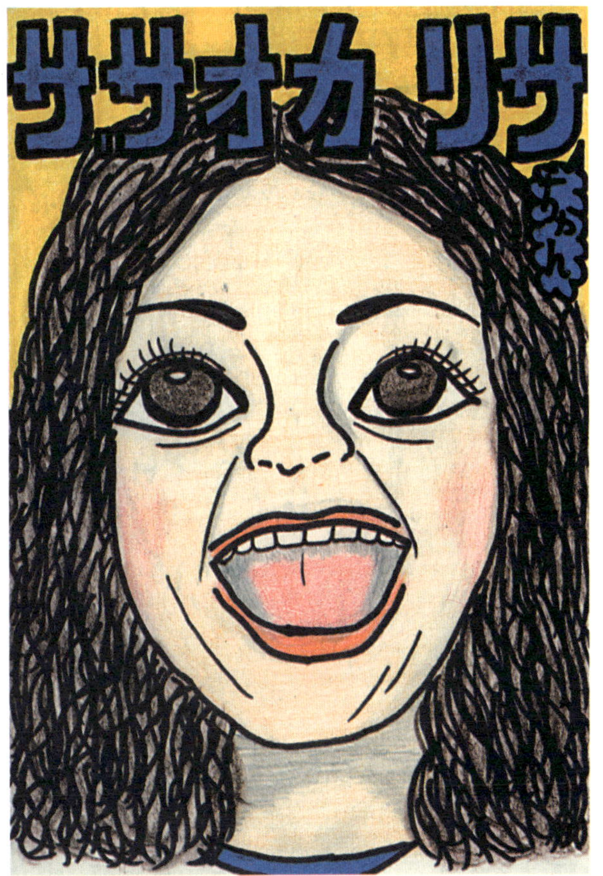

Risa Sasaoka

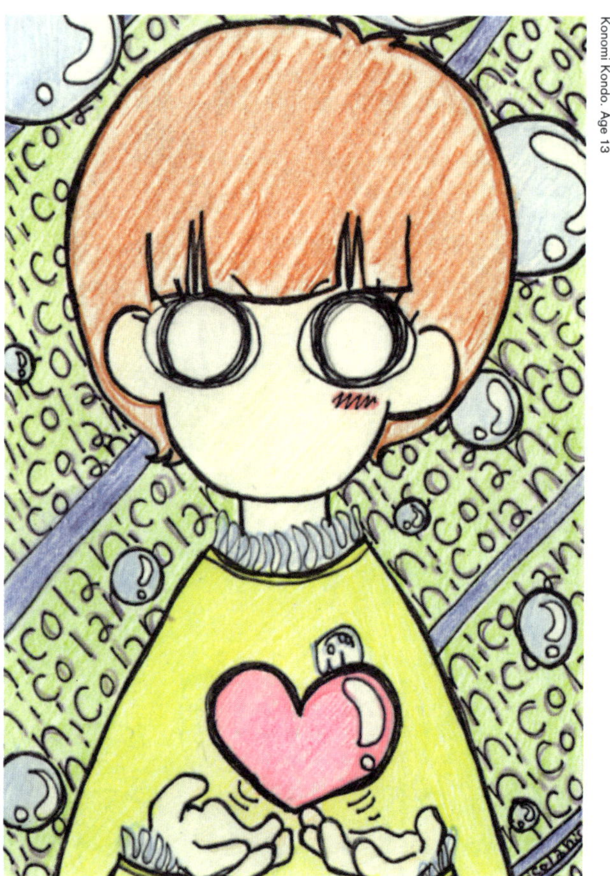

Konomi Kondo. Age 13

Peritora. Age 12

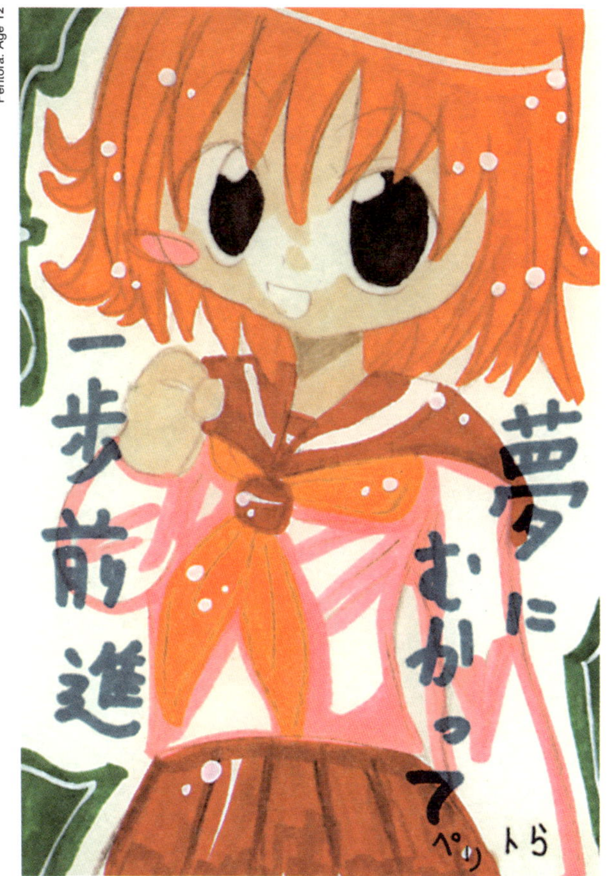

Step toward your dreams.

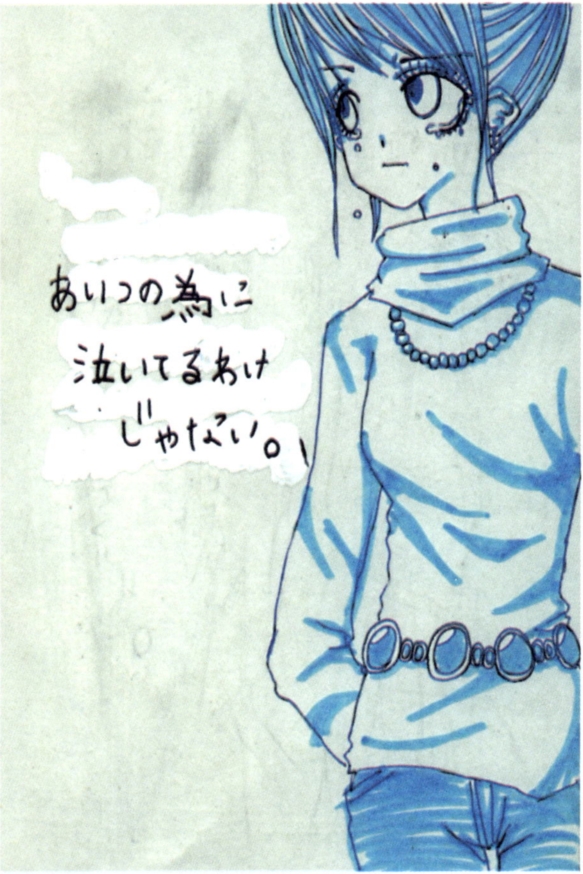

あいつの為に
泣いてるわけ
じゃない。

Momoiro Ichigo (Marisu Minazuki). Age 15

"I'm not crying for him".

Yuuc. Age 13

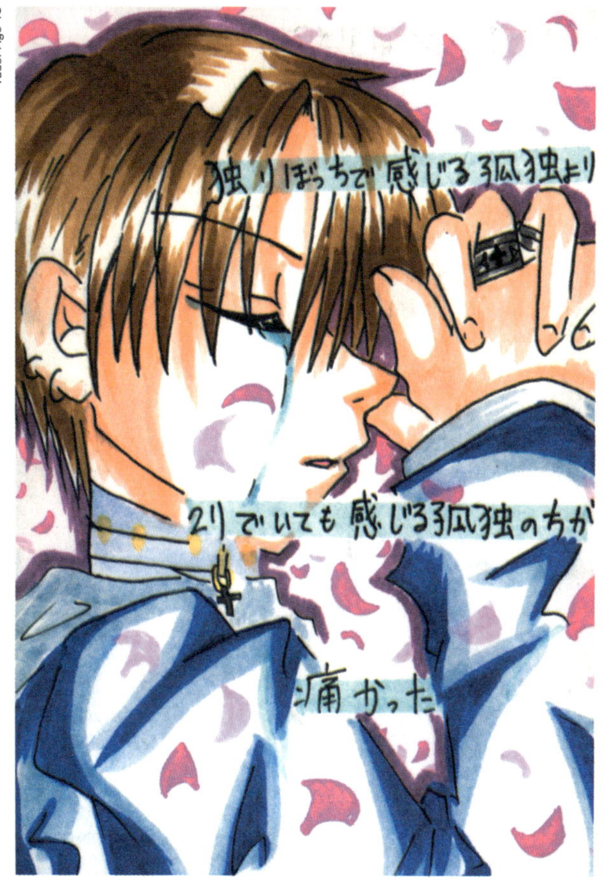

I felt more solitude with you more than when I was alone–it was painful.

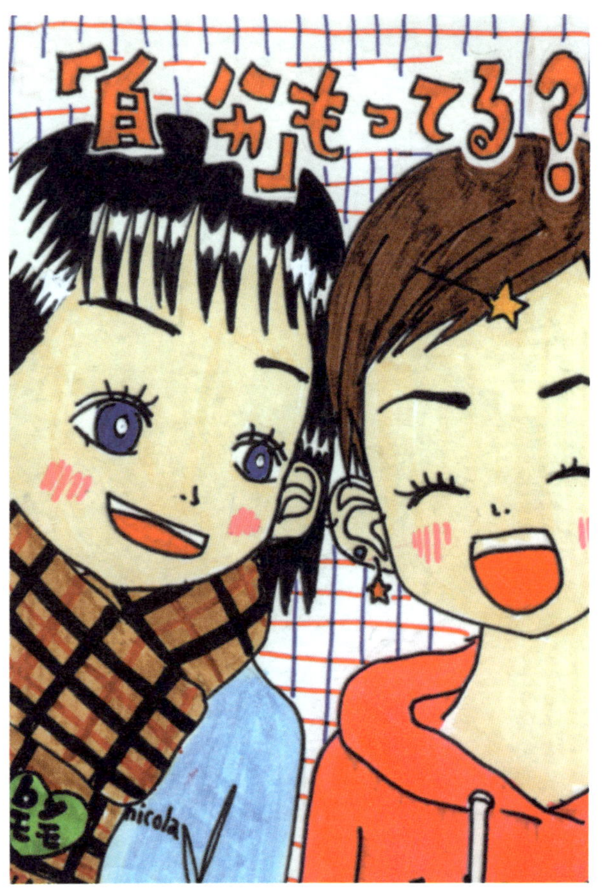

Momo. Age 13

Do you have “yourself”?

Natsu. Age 14

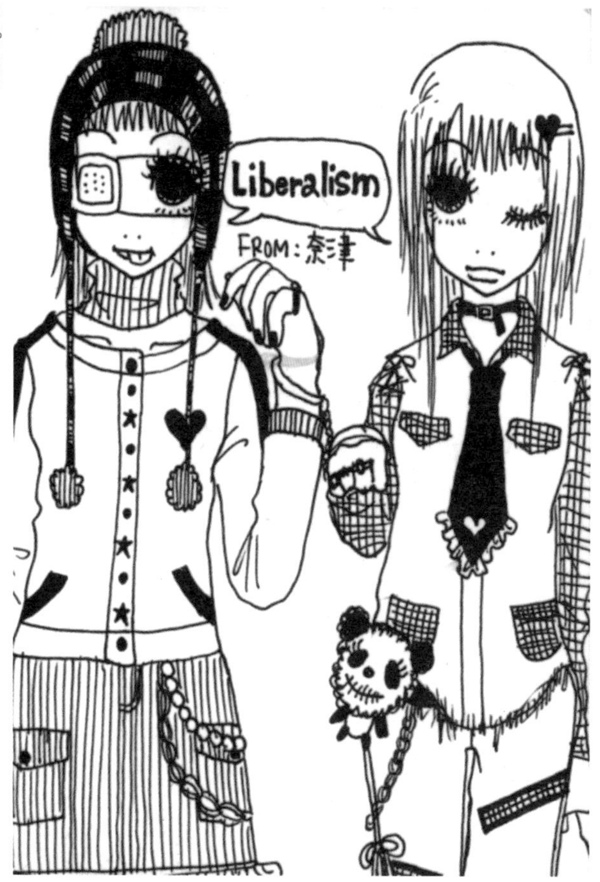

Liberalism

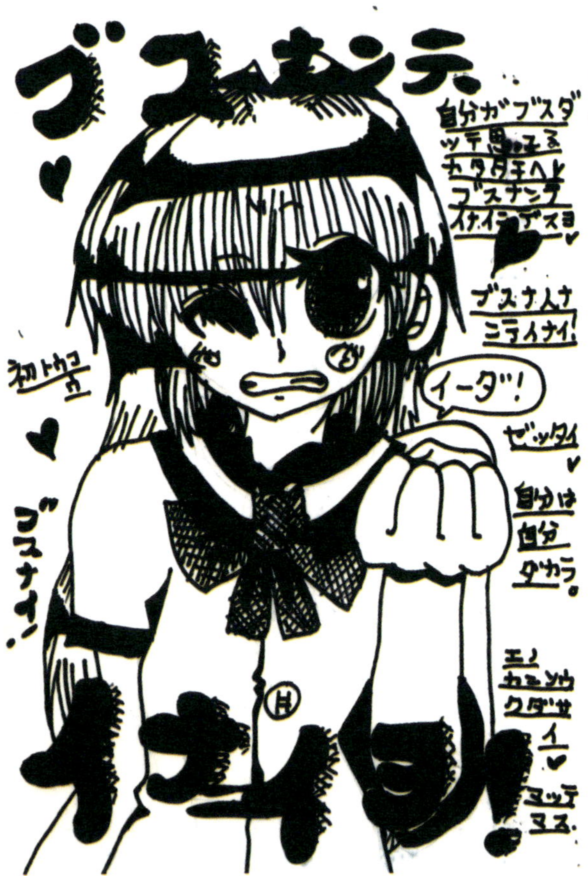

No one can be an ugiy girl!

Makiko Nakano. Age 12

Hika. Age 14

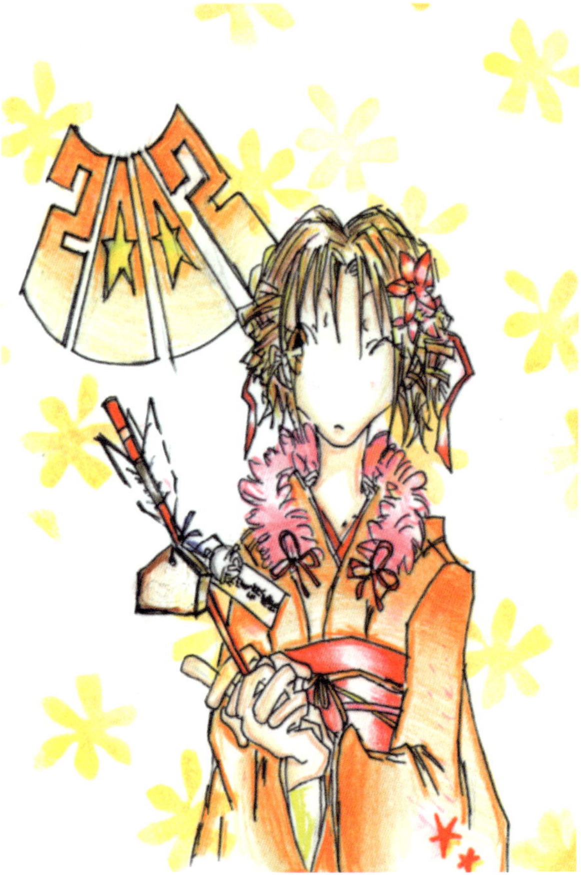

RAKI. Age 12

Awo. Age 12

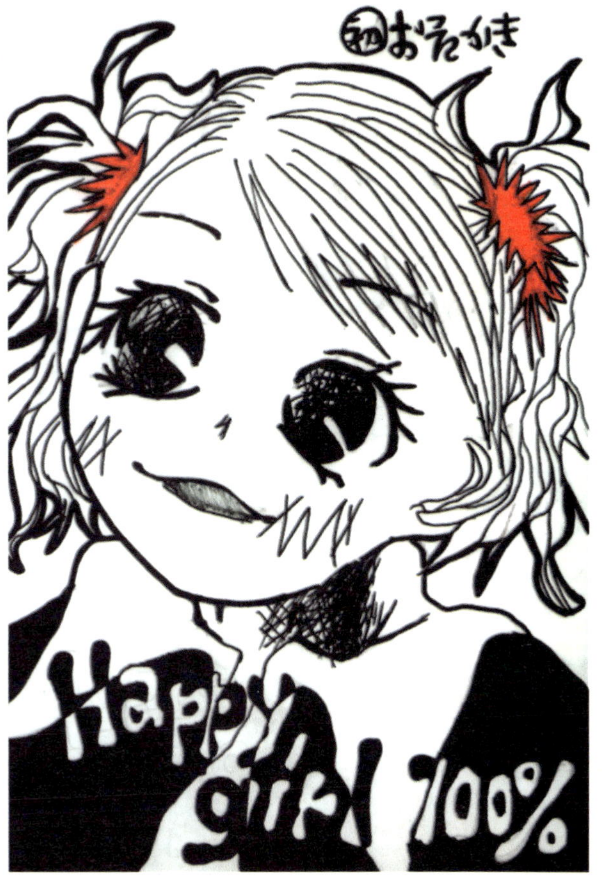

Happy girl 100%

Rio. Age 14

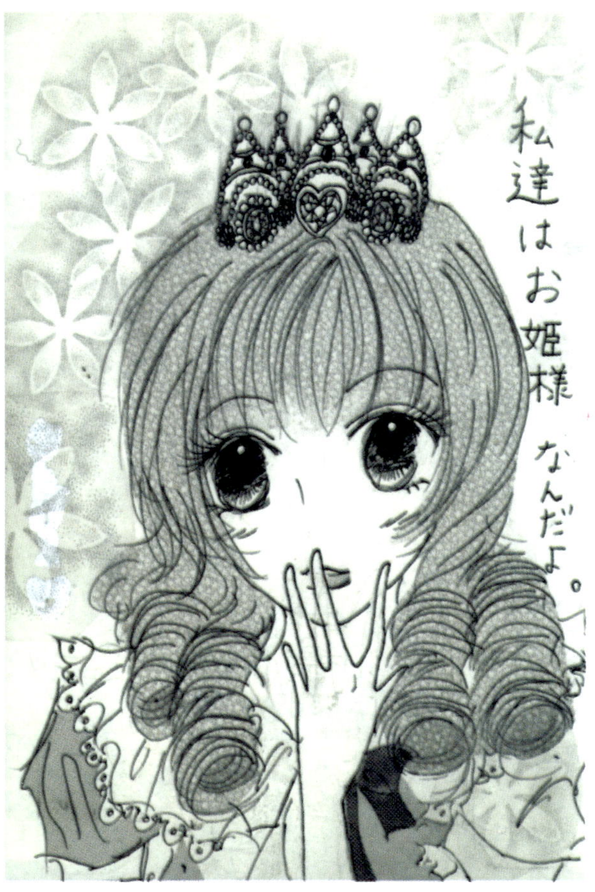

We are all princesses.

Minami Watanabe. Age 11

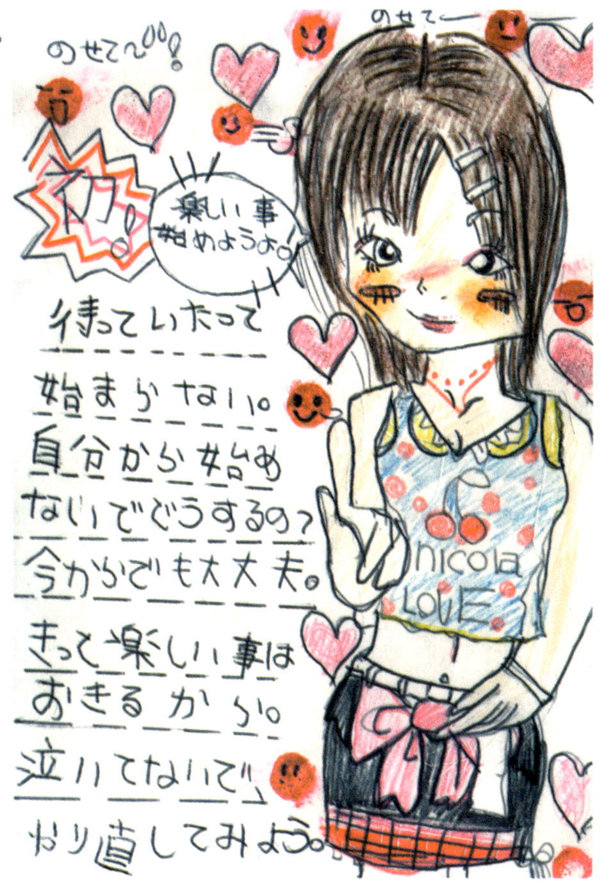

Let's start having fun! Nothing will happen if you are just waiting. Why don't you just try? It's not too late. And then something nice will happen. Don't cry, do try again!

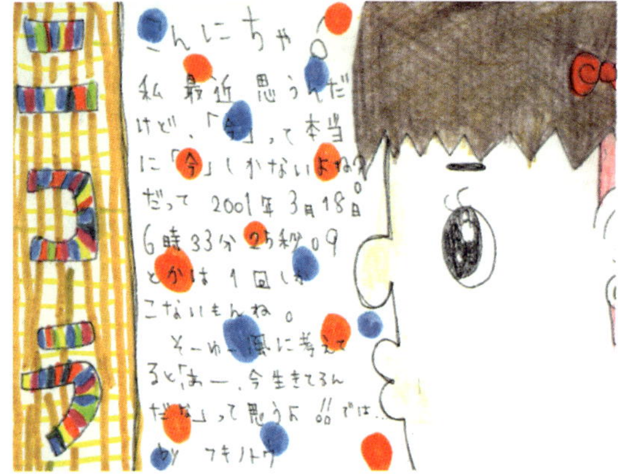

Fukinotou. Age 13

Recently, I've been thinking that "present time" is truly "now". On the date of 18th March 2001, the time of 6:33:25:09 came only once, never again. Therefore, I go "Wow, I am alive right now", always.

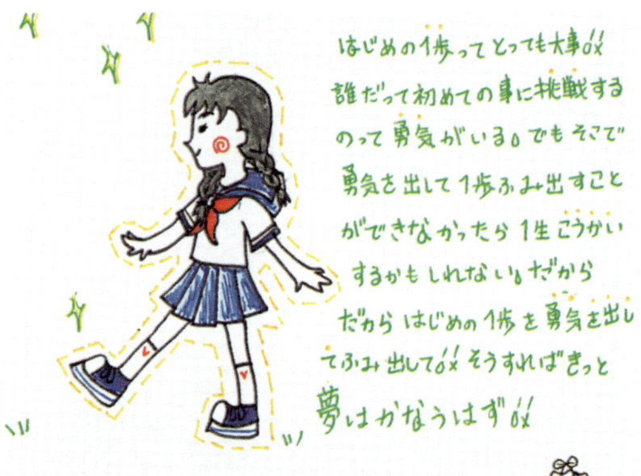

Blue Cherry. Age 13

The First Step. It's very important, the first step!! Anyone needs the courage to challenge the new thing. But if you can't do it now, you might regret it. So be brave to make the first step!!

Gonza. Age 13

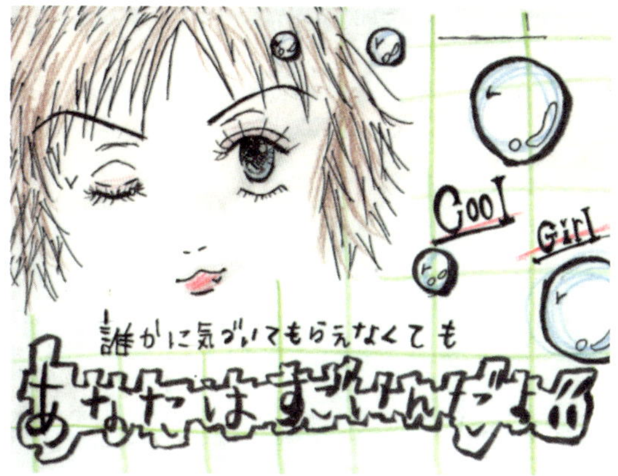

Even though nobody notices your attraction, you are great!!

Pika LOVE. Age 12

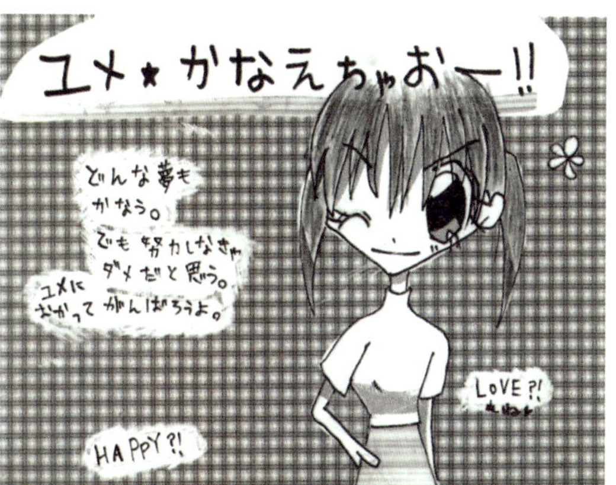

Let's try to make dreams come true!! Every dream will come true, but it needs effort. Let's do our best for dreams, also for loves, shall we?

Yui. Age 14

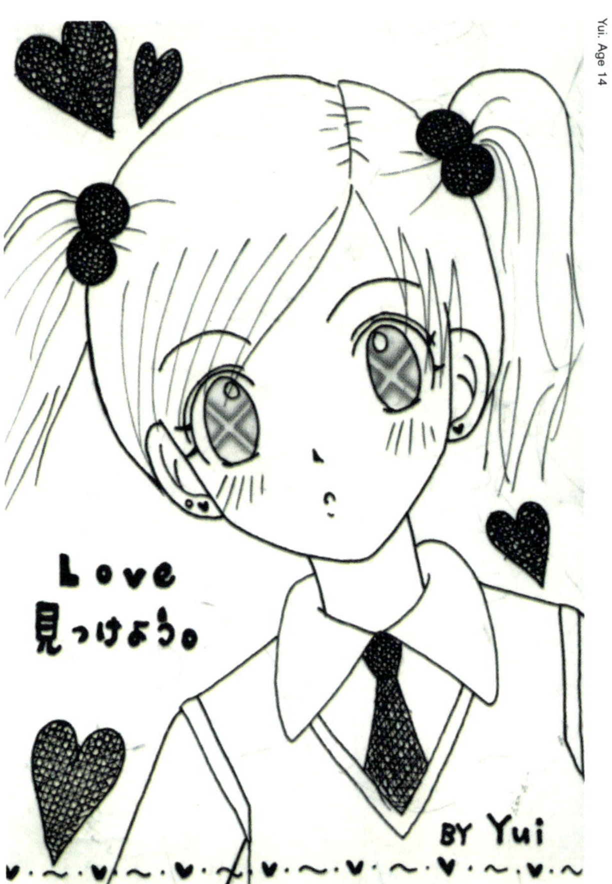

Let's find a love.

Mina. Age 14

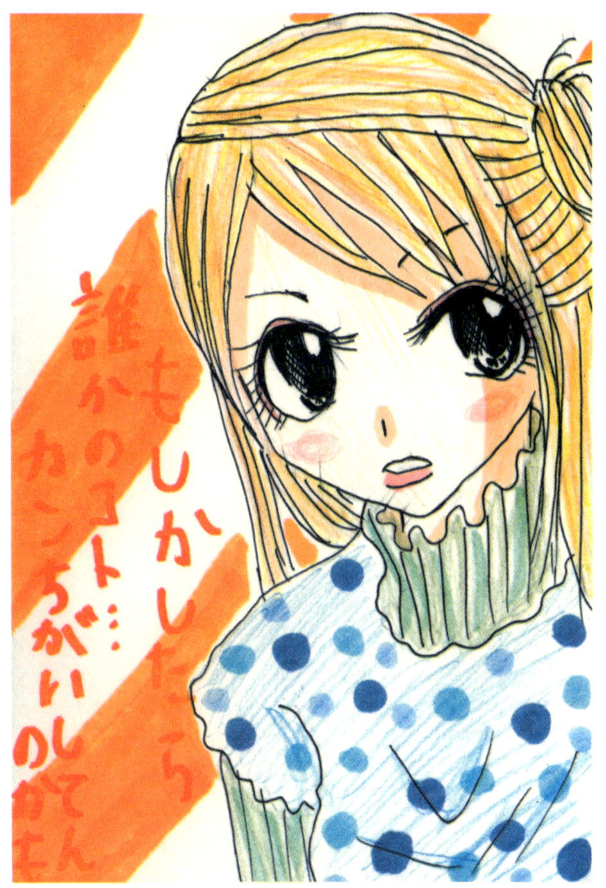

I might misunderstand someone's mind.

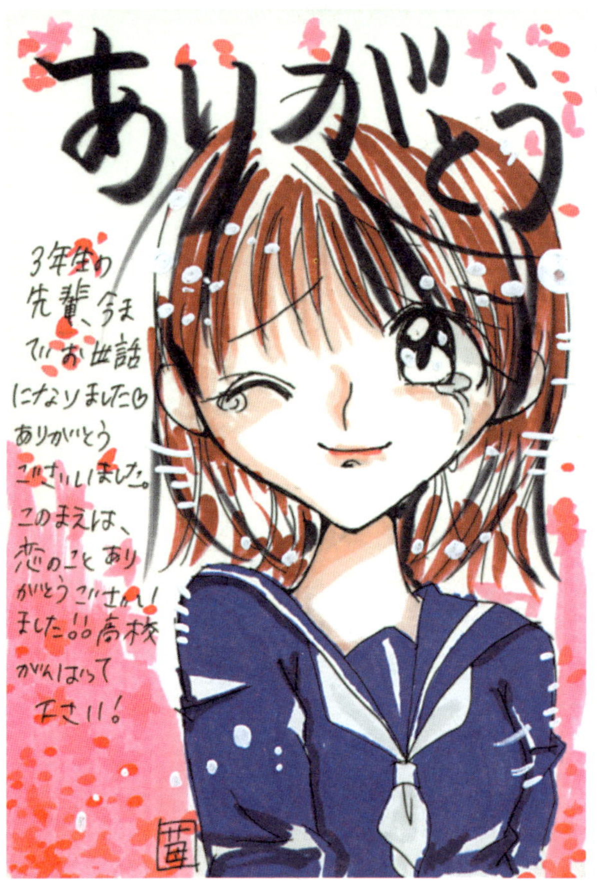

Harunanko. Age 14

Thank you.Thank you very much for listening to my love trouble!! Good luck in high school!

Koharu.

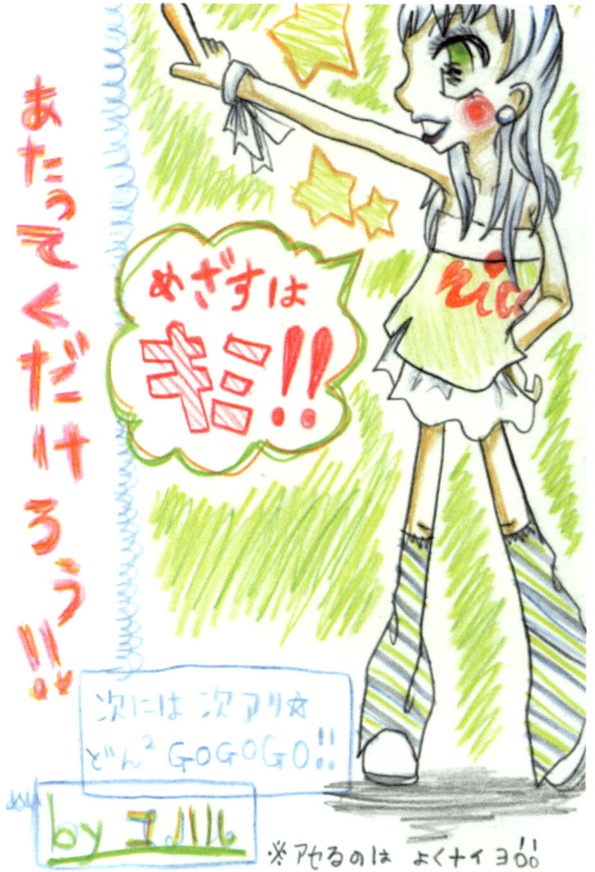

Take your chance! What I want is you!! Next please, c'mon go go go!! Don't get impatient!

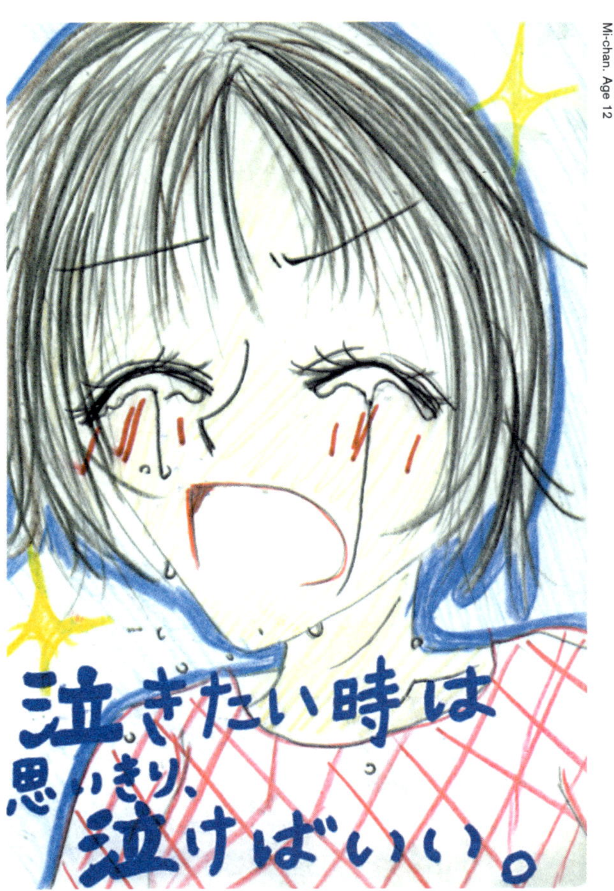

Mi-chan. Age 12

You can cry whenever you want.

Yu. Age 15

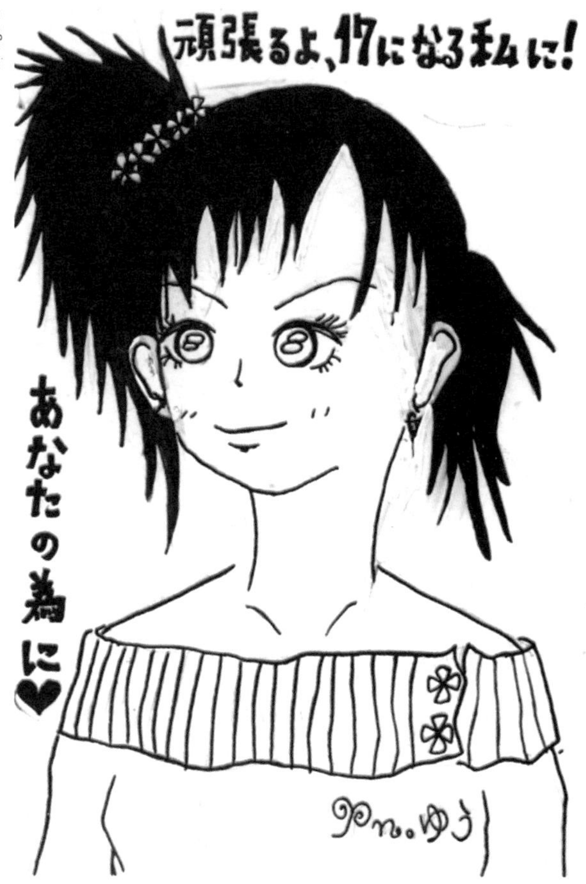

I'll do my best, I'm gonna be 17! For you.

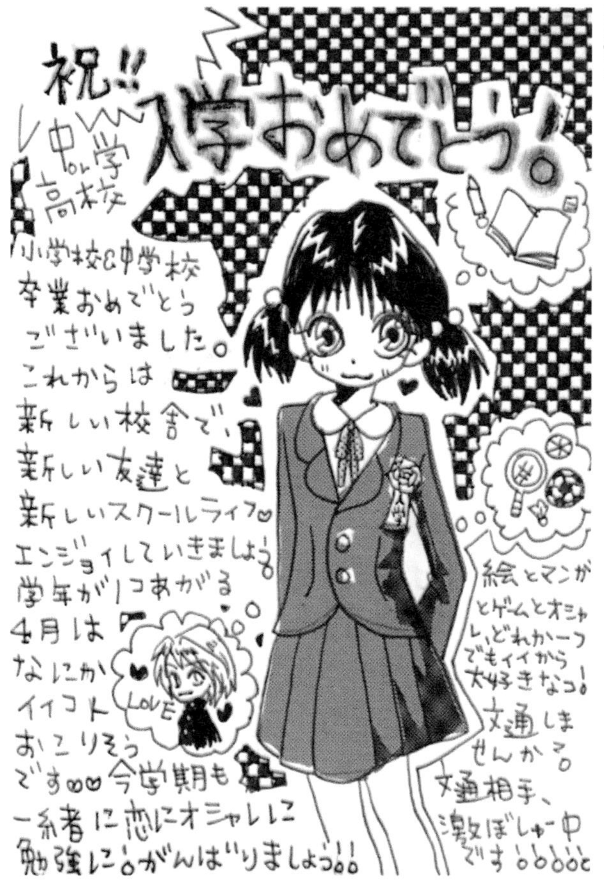

Uni. Age 12

Congratulations for the entrance into a school! Let's enjoy new school buildings! I feel something nice is going to happen. Let's enjoy love, fashion and studying!!

Saori. Age 12

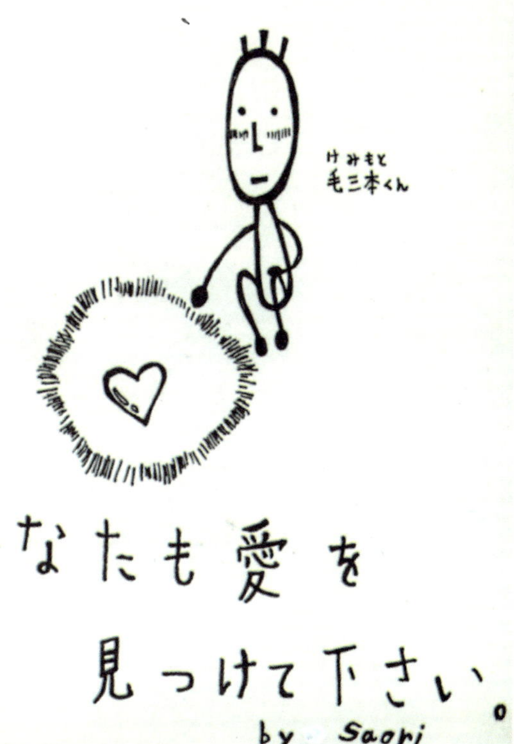

Please, you too can find a love. Mr.3 Hairs

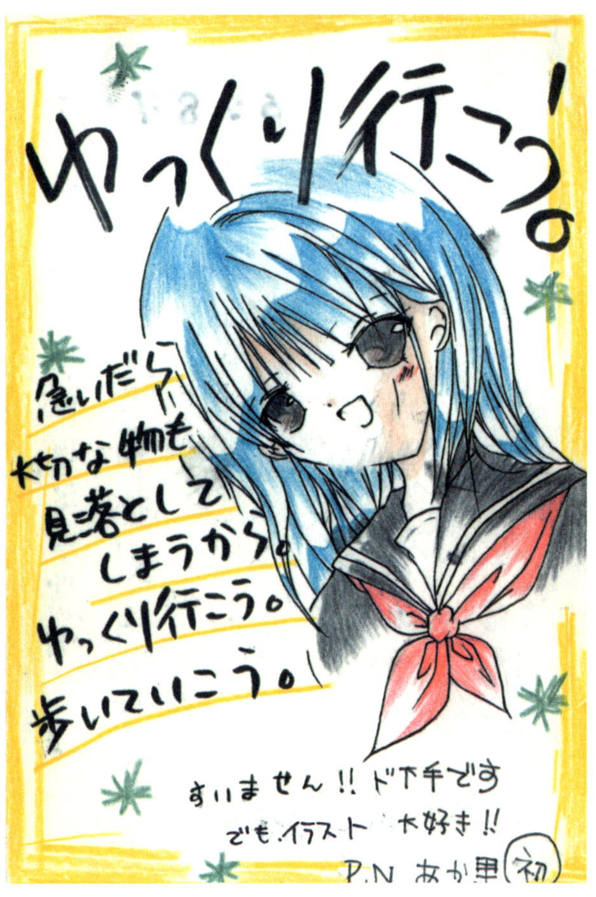

Akari. Age 12

Slowly! You will miss something important if you are in a hurry. Go slowly and keep walking.

Hikki-❤. Age 15

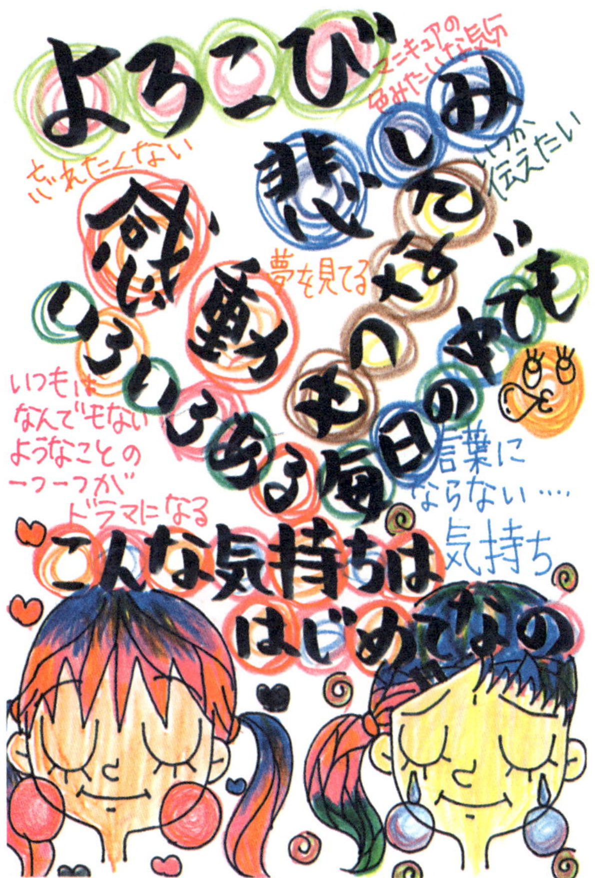

Joy, sadness, deep emotion, ardentness. I find a lot in daily life. I never felt like this before. I don't want to forget the feelings like colours of nail enamel. I'm dreaming. I want to tell somebody some day. Feelings beyond words. Everything is turning into a drama.

Lulu.

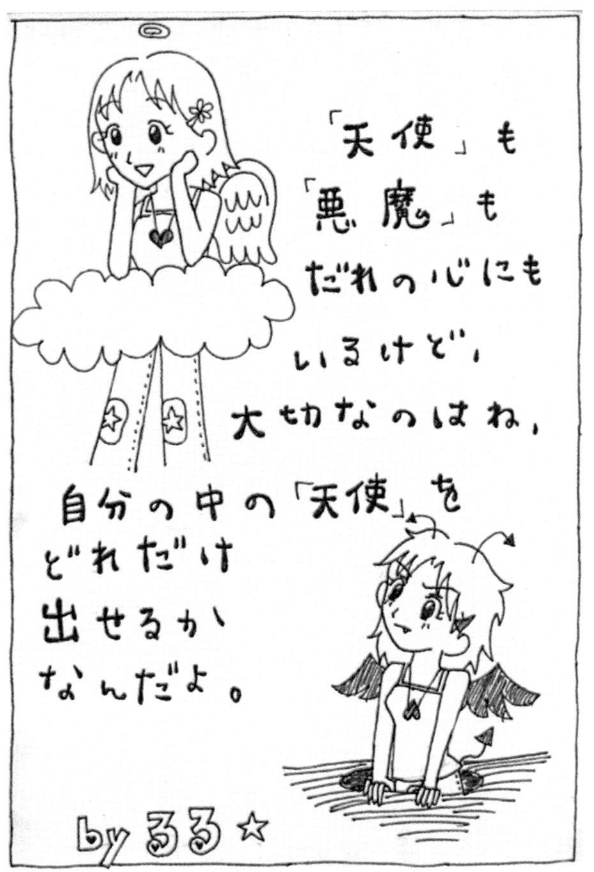

Everyone has got an angel and evil in the heart, but the important thing is, how much you can find an angel in you?

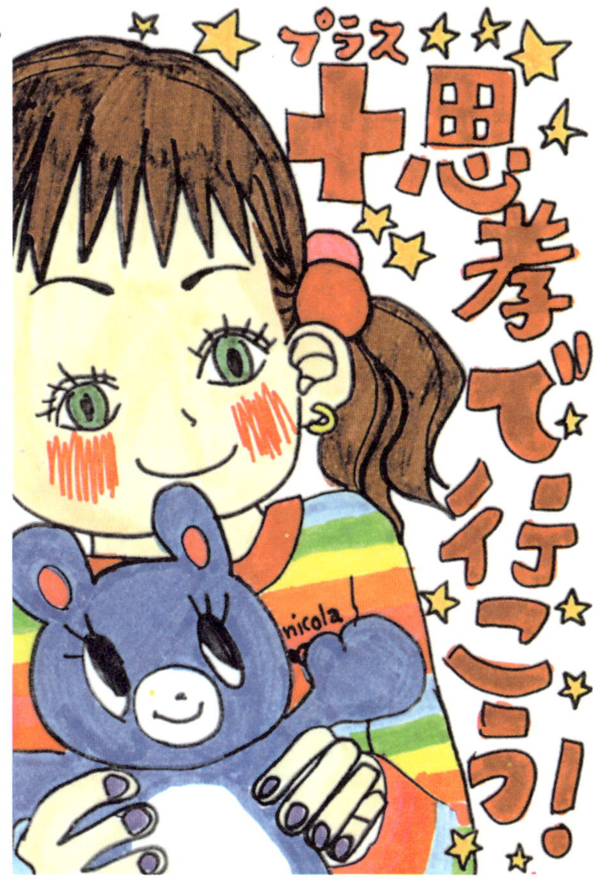

Momo. Age 13

Be positive!

Tomoko. Age 13

DREAM

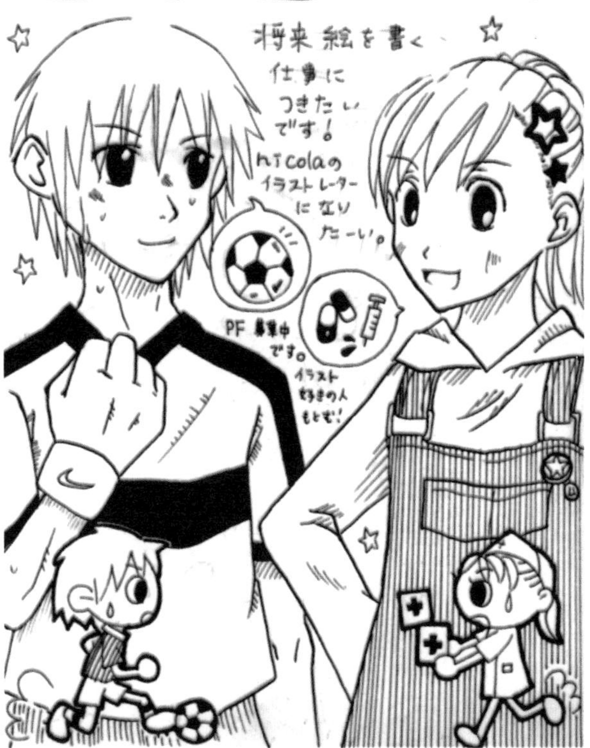

My dream job is an illustrator. I wanna work for " Nicola."

Chili Ame. Age 14

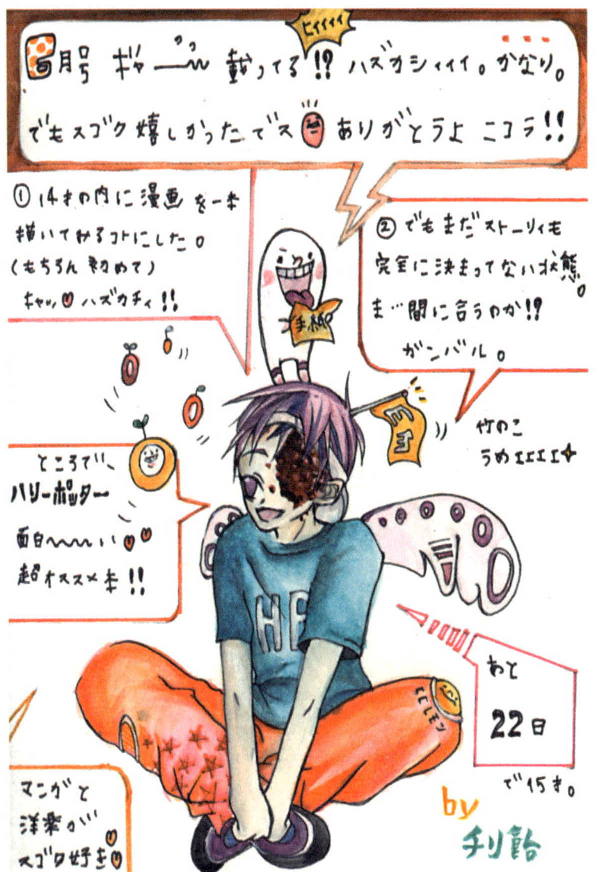

1. I am making my first cartoon while being 14 years old. Wow, I'm embarassed!! 2. I haven't determined the story completely yet though. Can I finish it up before my 15th birthday? I have only 22days left for it…

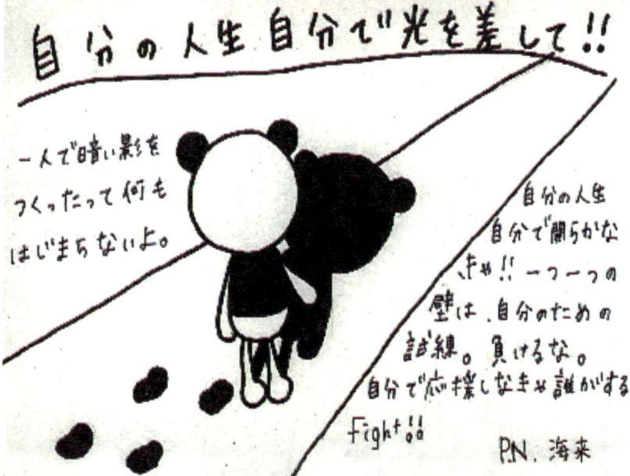

Miko. Age 13

Give a focus on your own life!! No point creating a dark shadow. Create your own life!! Each obstacle lies for yourself. Don't be a loser. Who supports you if you don't!!

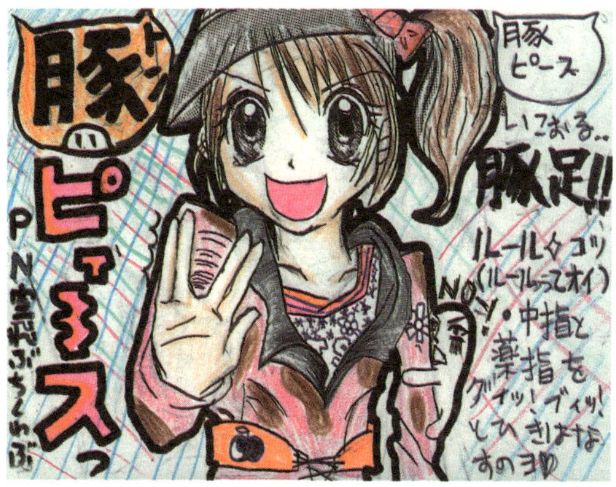

Soratobu Chikuwabu. Age 12

The pig peace sign. The pig peace equals a pig foot! The way to make the pig peace sign: separate your middle and third finger as much as possible! Gui Bui!!

Chikuwa musume. Age 12

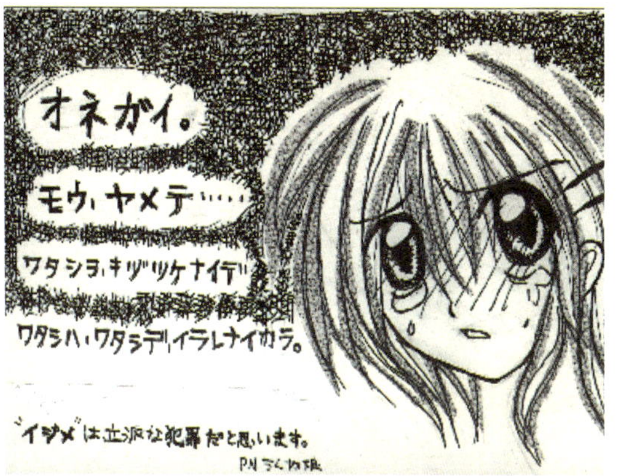

Please, don't do it any more…Please don't hurt me because I cannot be myself. I think bullying is a serious crime.

Yuine Aihara. Age 13

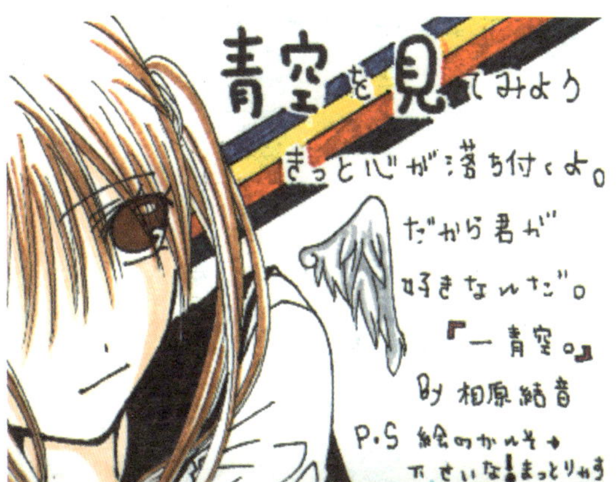

Look up the blue sky. It makes you relax. That's why I like you.
"—— Blue sky."

WHY DON'T SHOW ME real oneself

ドウシテ本当の自分を見せないの？

by 六月恵子

Why don't you show me the real you?

Keiko Rokugatsu, Age 15

Miyabi Kimura. Age 15

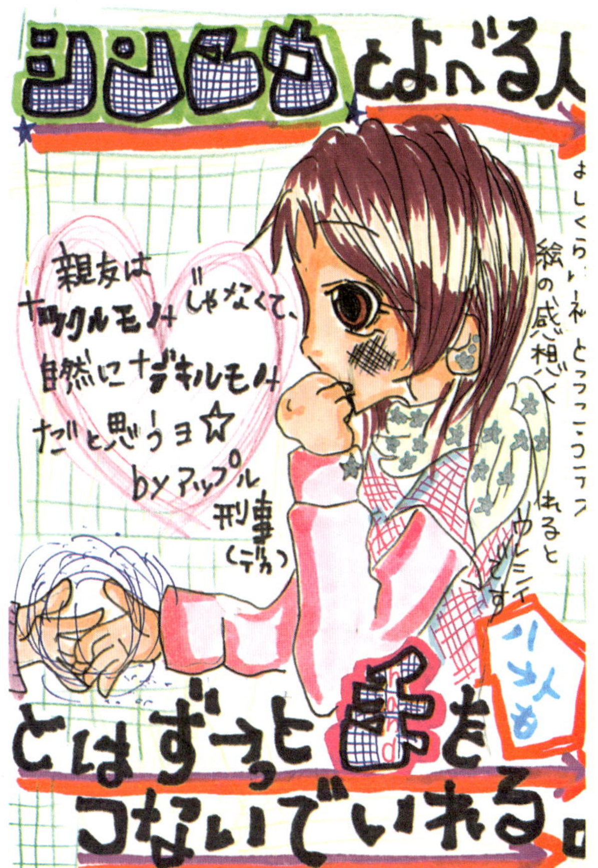

I can keep holding my best friend's hand forever. I think you just need to 'be' a friend, not to 'make' a friend. By Apple Cop

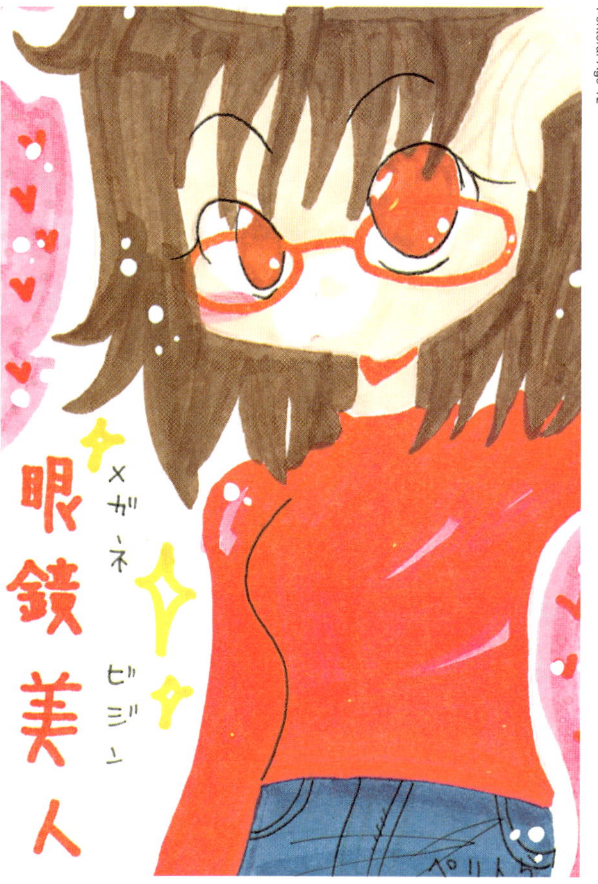

Peritora. Age 12

A beauty with glasses.

Peritora. Age 12

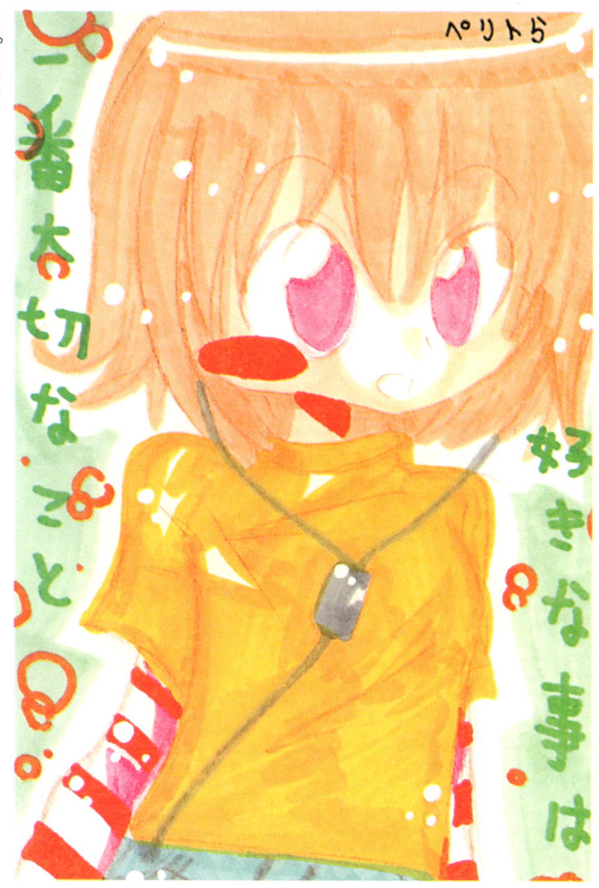

What you like is the most important thing.

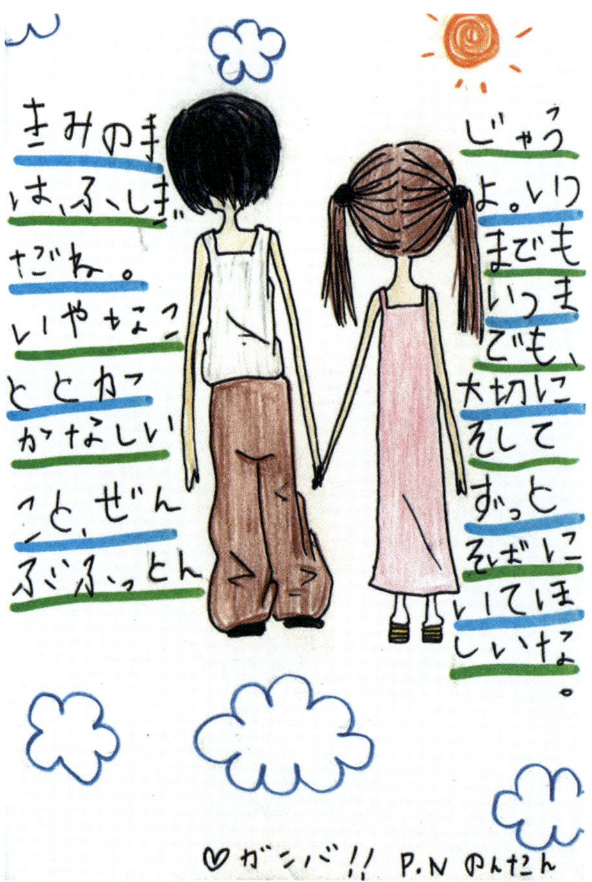

Your hand is wonderful. It blows away all sad horrible things. I want you to stay by me forever, caring for each other.

Nontan.

Ahiru.

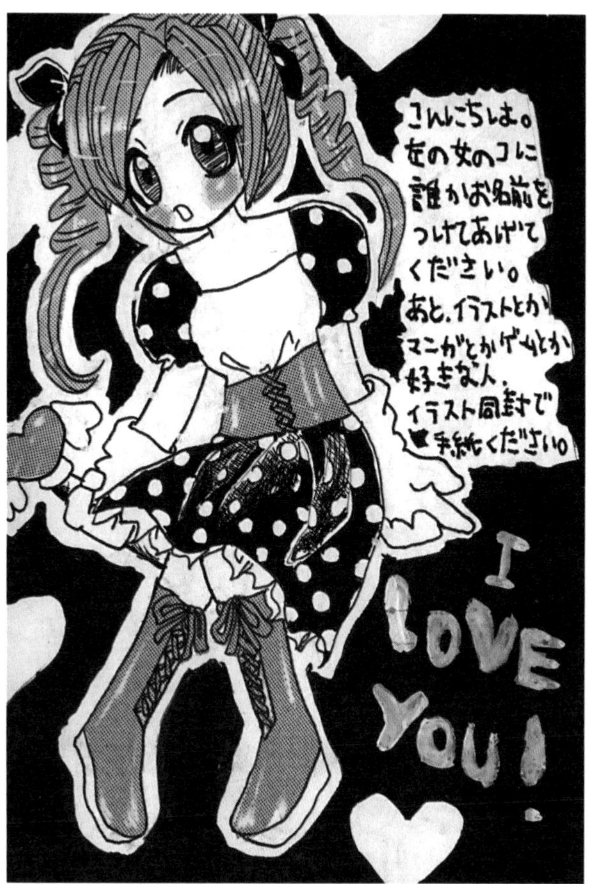

Hello. Please give her a name.

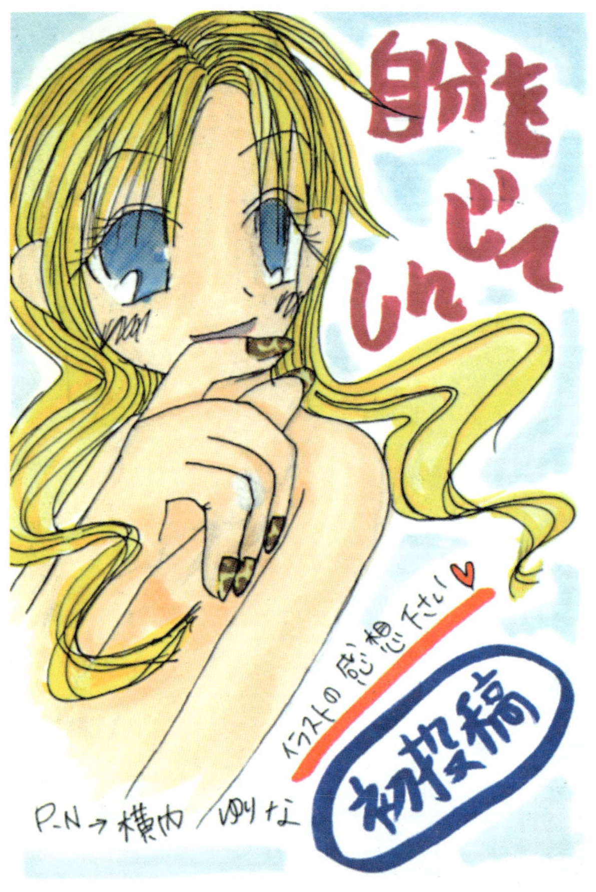

Yurina Yokouchi. Age 14

Believe yourself.

Mai. Age 14

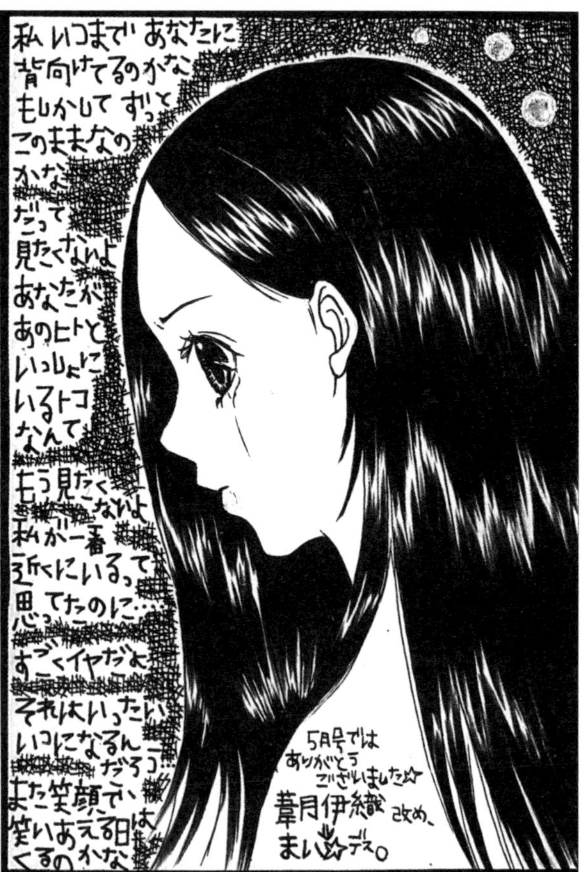

How long do I have to stay away from you? Forever? I don't want to see you with that girl. No more. I thought it was me who was the closest to you… I can't take this. When can we smile each other again?

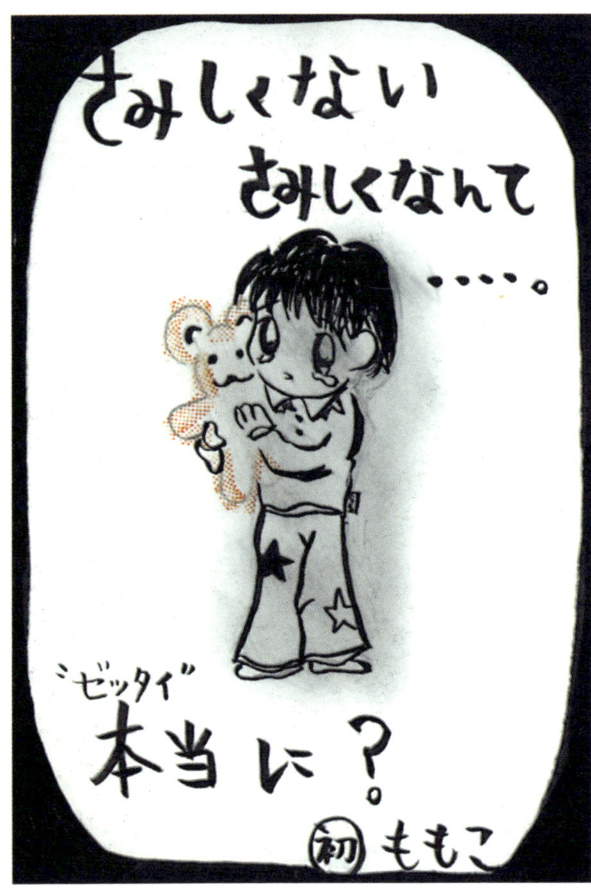

Momoko. Age 14

I'm not lonely, I'm not…
Really?

Mai. Age 11

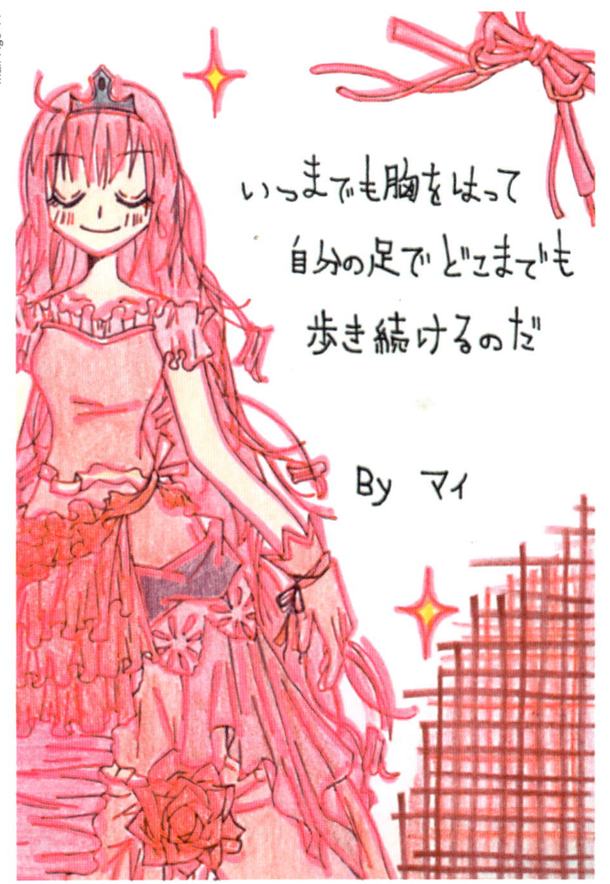

I'll stand proud and keep walking with my feet forever.

Mikan Guratan. Age 12

自分が大好き。

自分がキライな人に言いたいのです!!ブスだから…とか"キラわれているから…とか思っていると自分がかわいそうだよ!!もっと自分に自信をもって進んで行こう!!道は1つじゃないのだぁ

ガンバレ!!

人生

みかんグラタンより。

I love myself. I want to tell this to the girl who doesn't love herself. Its so sad if you think that you are ugly or nobody likes you!! Be more confident in yourself. There is more than one way in your life!!

Sho.

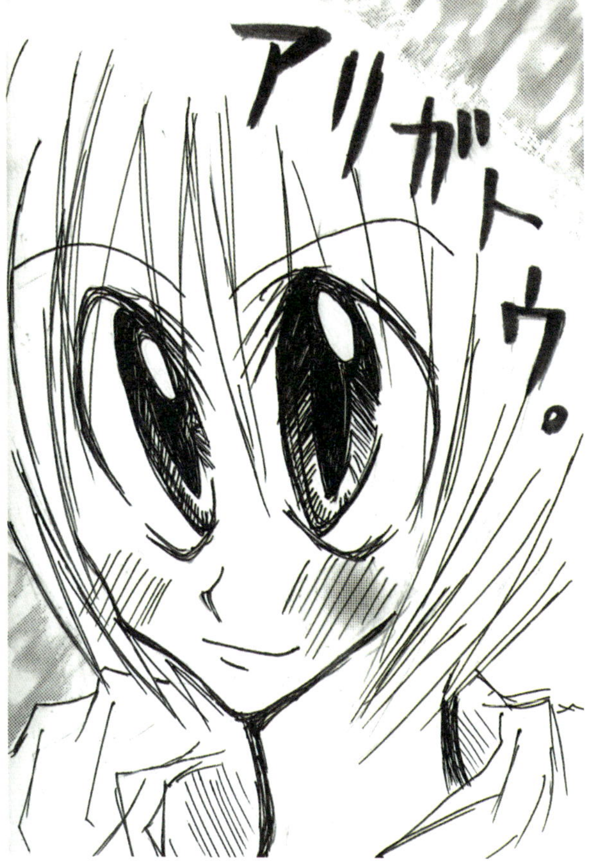

Thank you.

Mita. Age 12

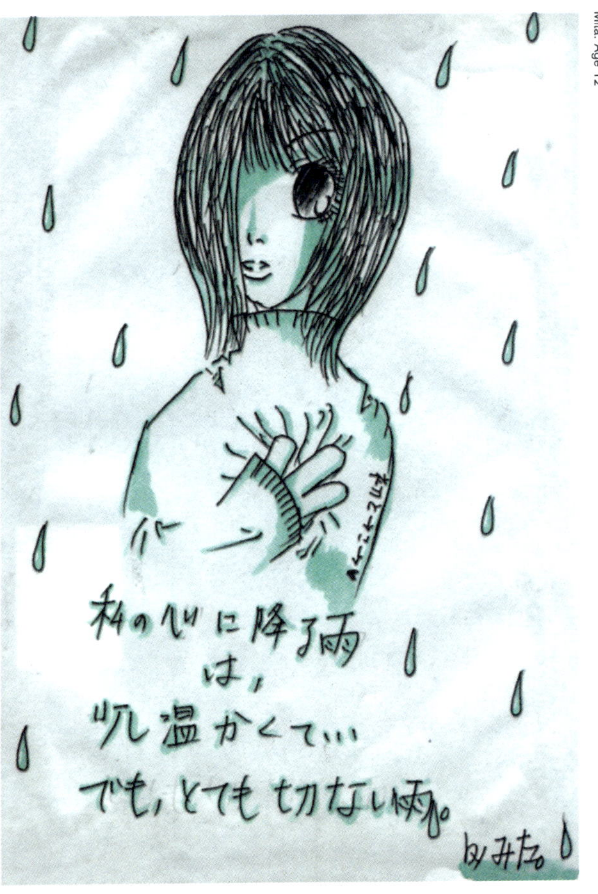

The rain which falls onto my heart is slightly warm and very sad.

Hirame Yogigen. Age 13

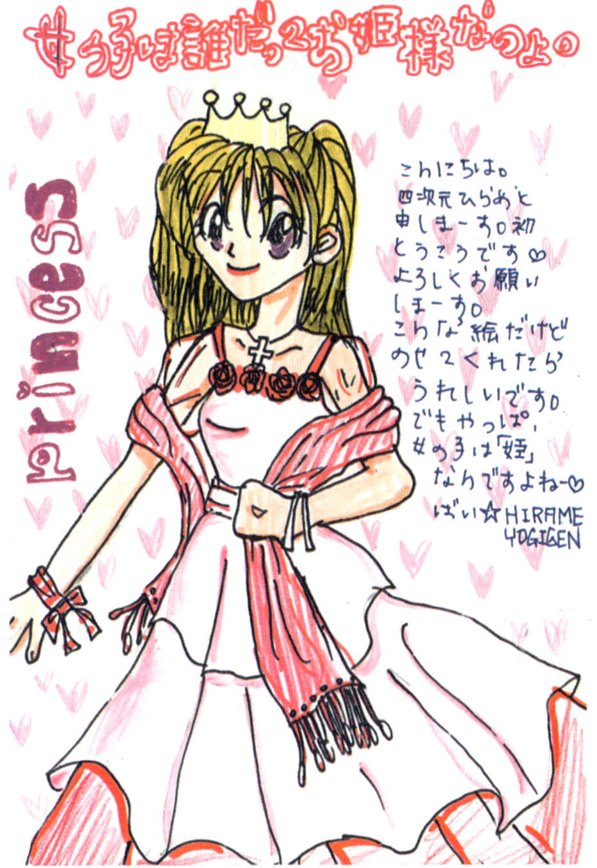

Every girl is a princess.

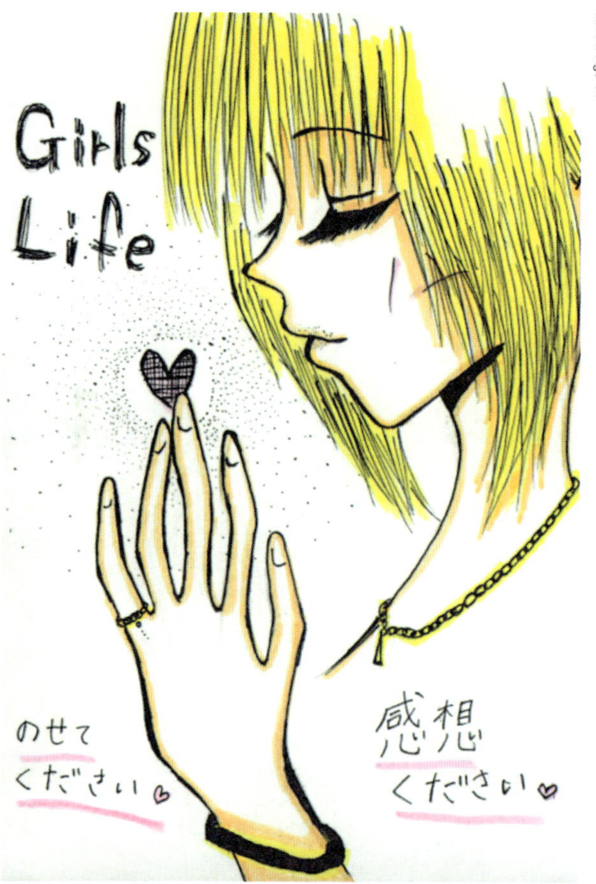

KITTY, Age 14

Please publish this postcard and send your comments about my drawing.

Sakura. Age 15

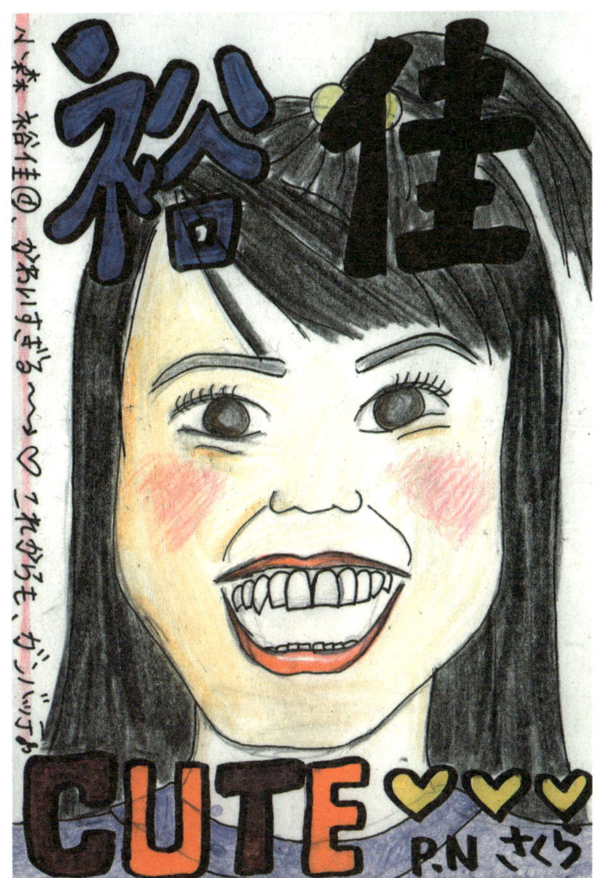

Yuka...She's too cute. Keep working hard.

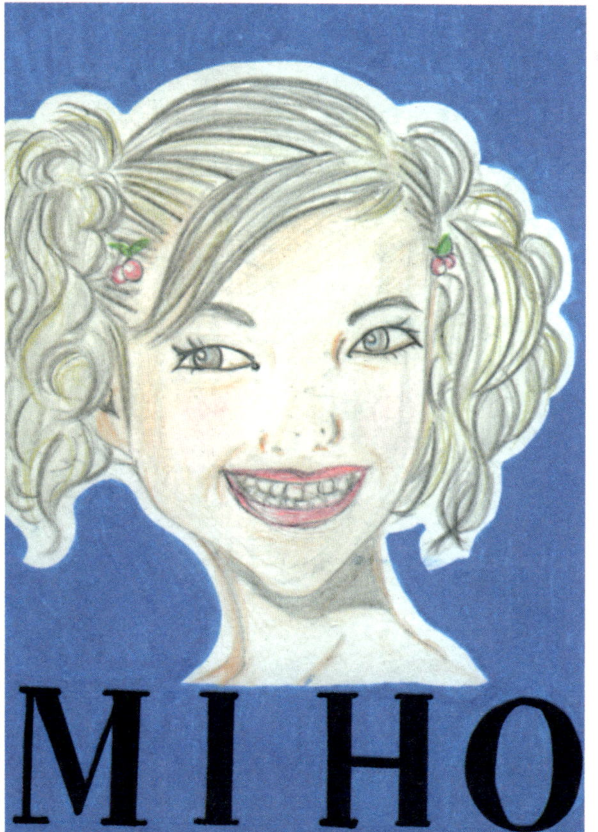

Kaori. Age 13

SKT. Age 15

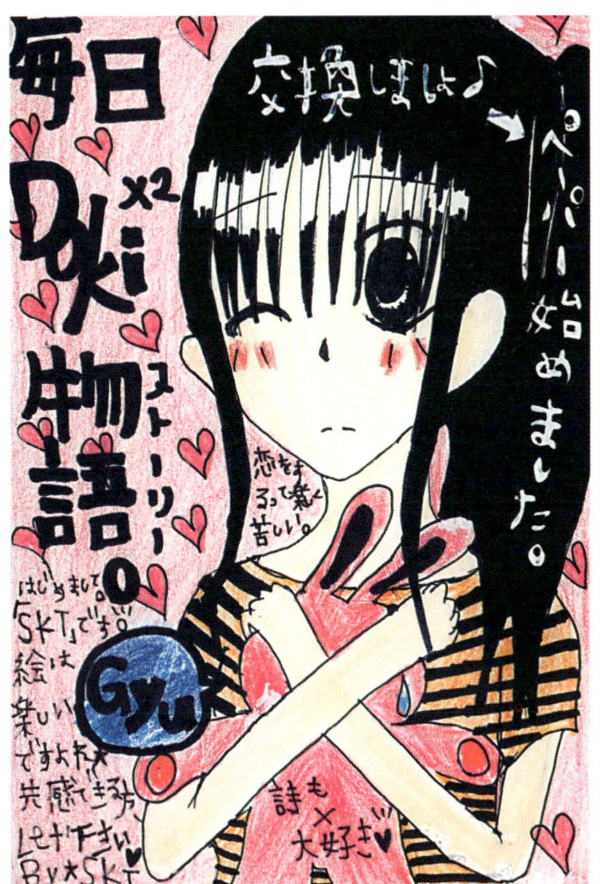

My heart has been beating everyday. Loving is joyful, but on the other hand it's painful.

Peritora. Age 12

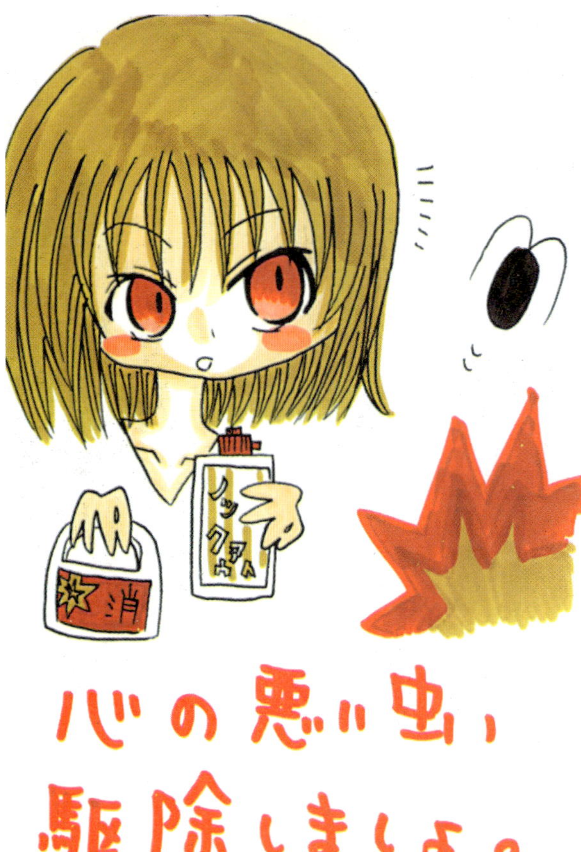

Let's get rid of bad bugs in our minds.

Peritora. Age 12

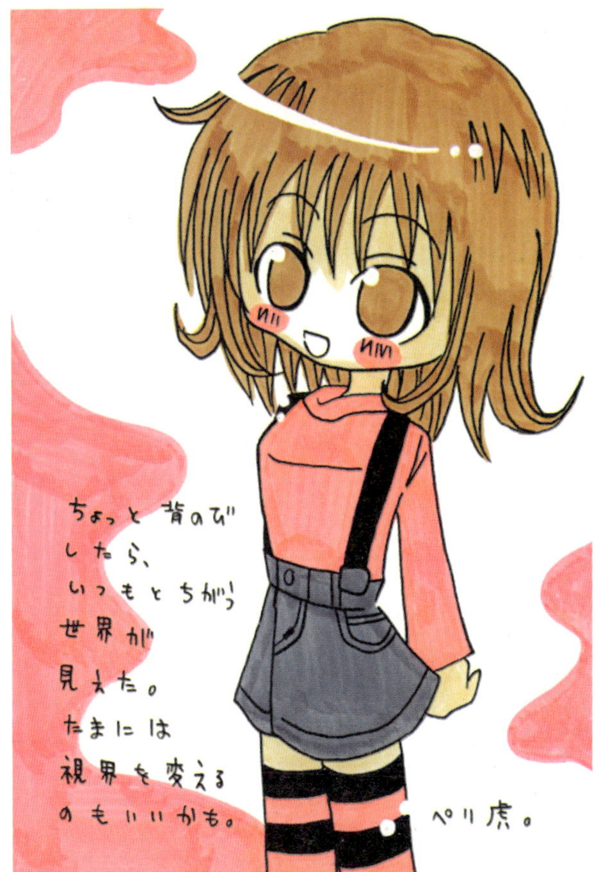

Standing on my tiptoes, I saw a different world from usual. Maybe it's a good idea to change your point of view.

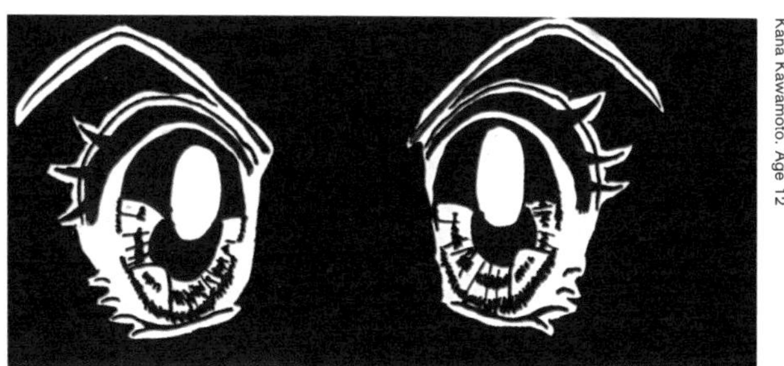

ライバルに

VS

ネイト－コー

負けるな！

感想ください♥

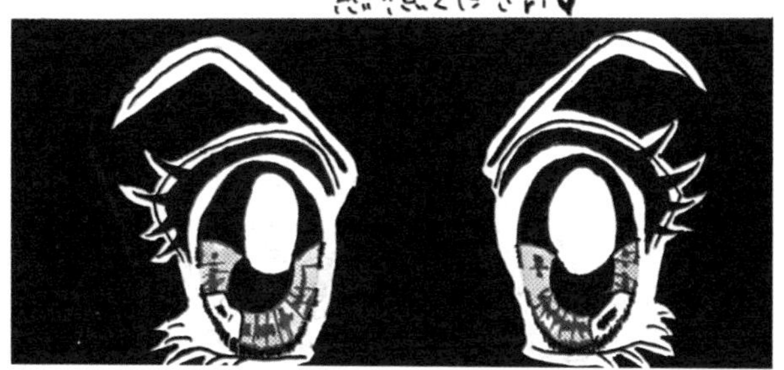

Don't be a loser

Kana Kawamoto. Age 12

605G. Age 14

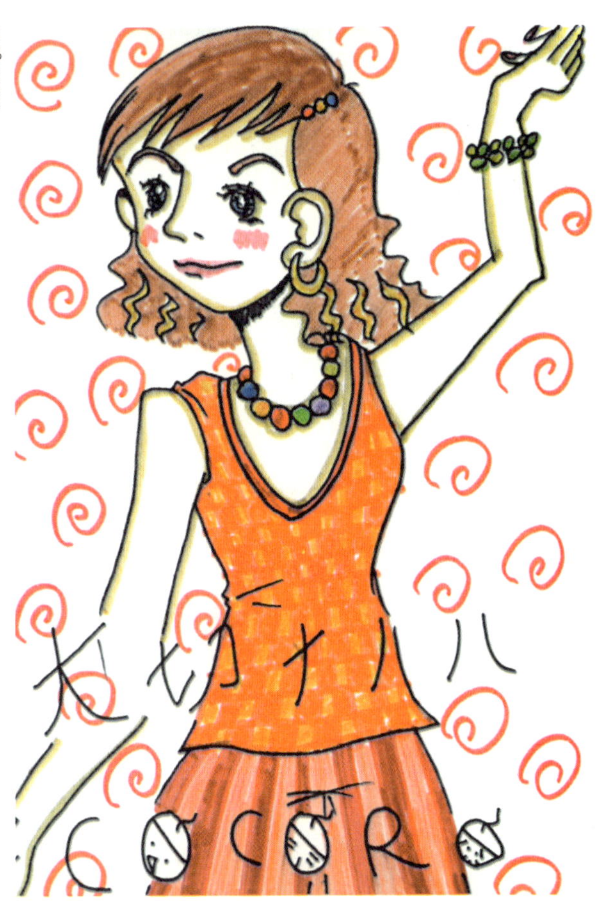

The most precious thing is the heart.

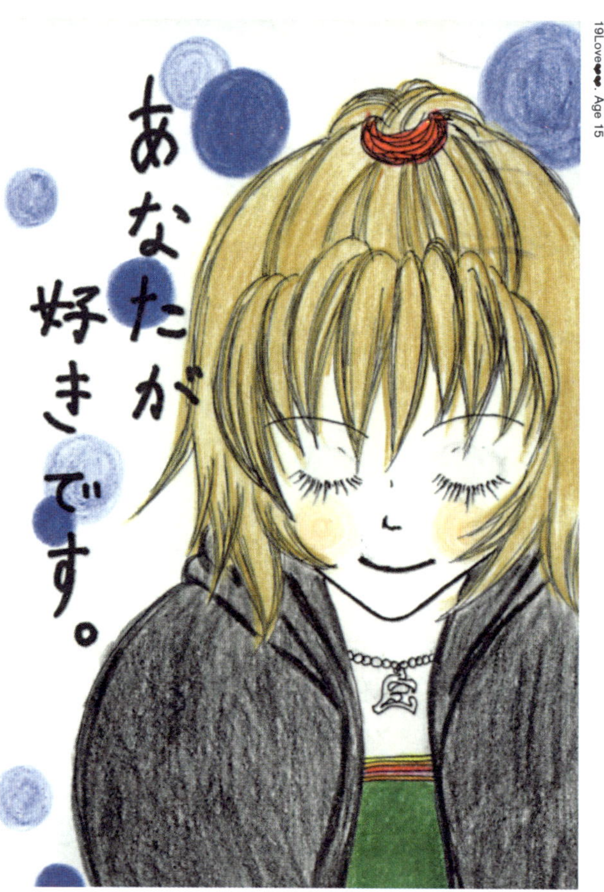

19Love❤❤. Age 15

I love you.

2001. Age 13

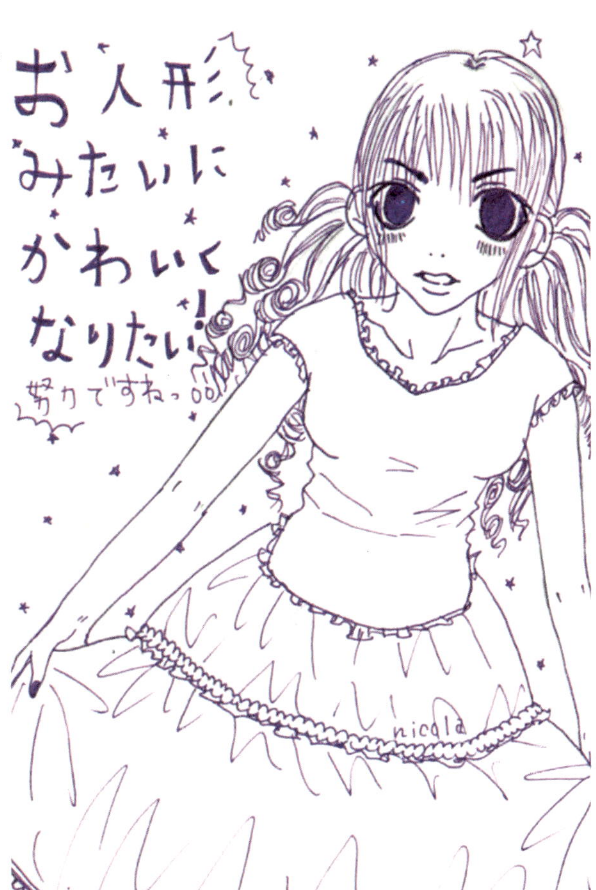

Wanna be a cute girl like a doll! Make an effort!

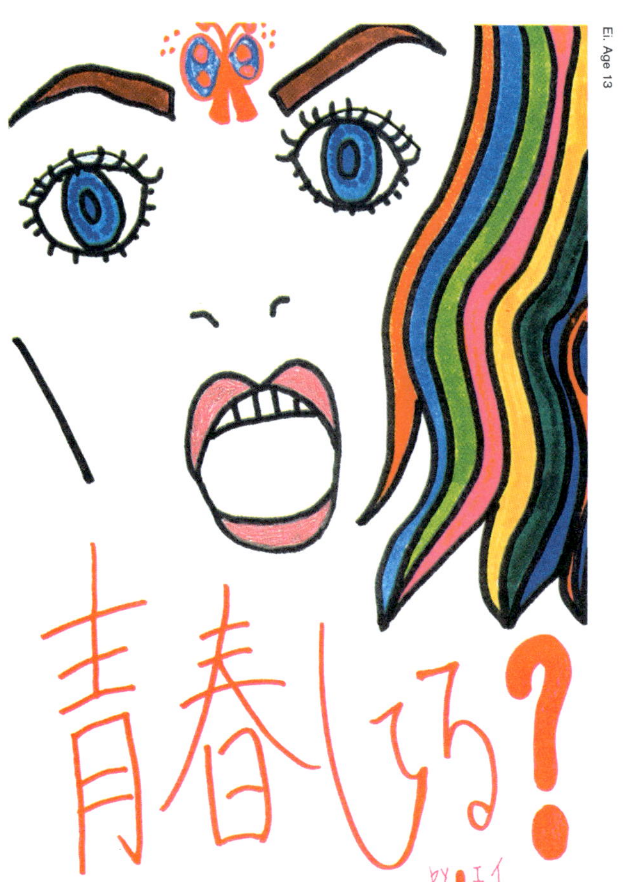

Ei. Age 13

Enjoying your youth?

Saori. Age 12

走って

走って

つかれたら

たまには

休んで

いいんだよ

いそぎすぎて

まわりを

みうしなったら

自分自身も みうしなうよ…

一息ついて

心も体も 休めよう

foo…

毛三本くん

by Saori

You keep running. Try to have a rest sometimes if you get tired. If you rush too much, you would miss something around you, then you'd lose your mind… Take a break, take care of your body and mind. Mr. 3 Hairs

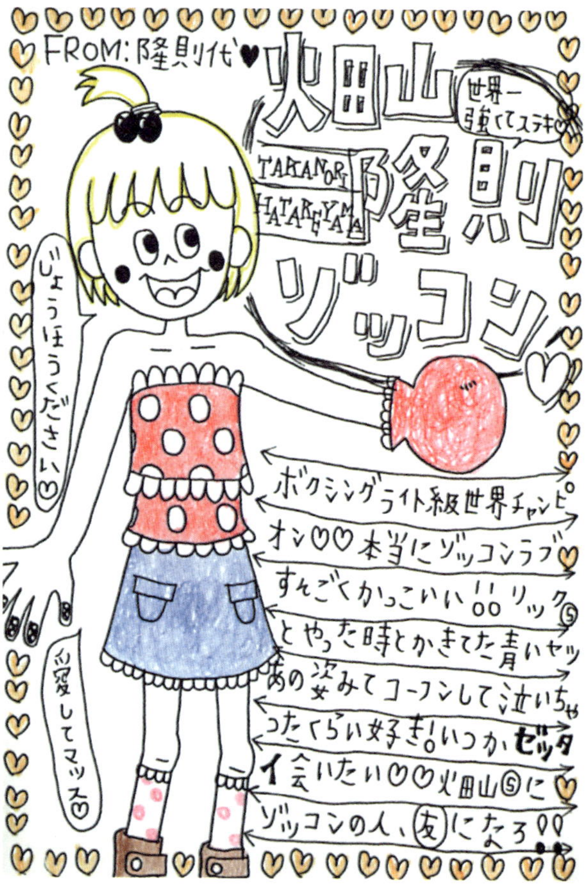

I'm crazy about Takanori Hatakeyama, the world champion of light class. When he had a match with Rick, he wore blue cloth that made me cry. You know how much I love him? Wanna meet him one day.

Maa Sakashita. Age 12

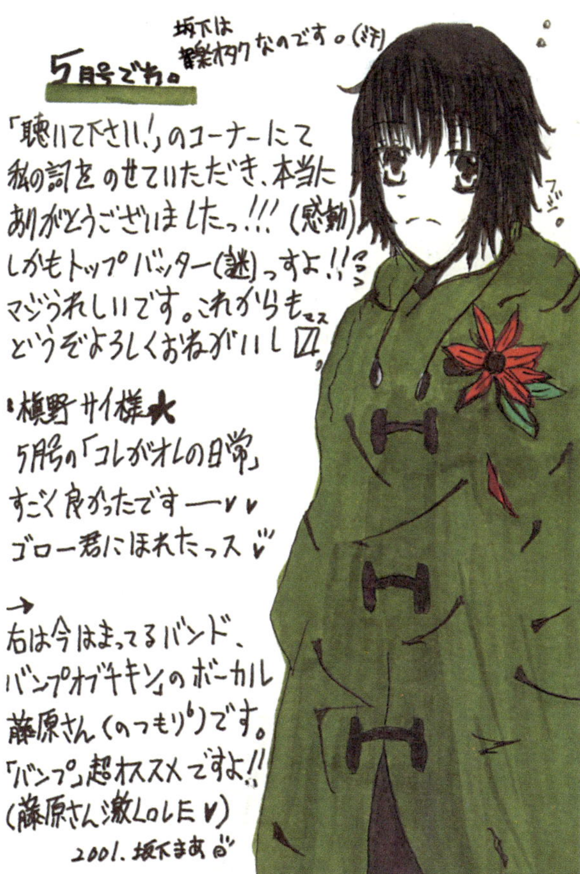

Thank you for introducing my poem!! I'm really into this band called "Bump of Chicken" Here is the vocalist of the band.

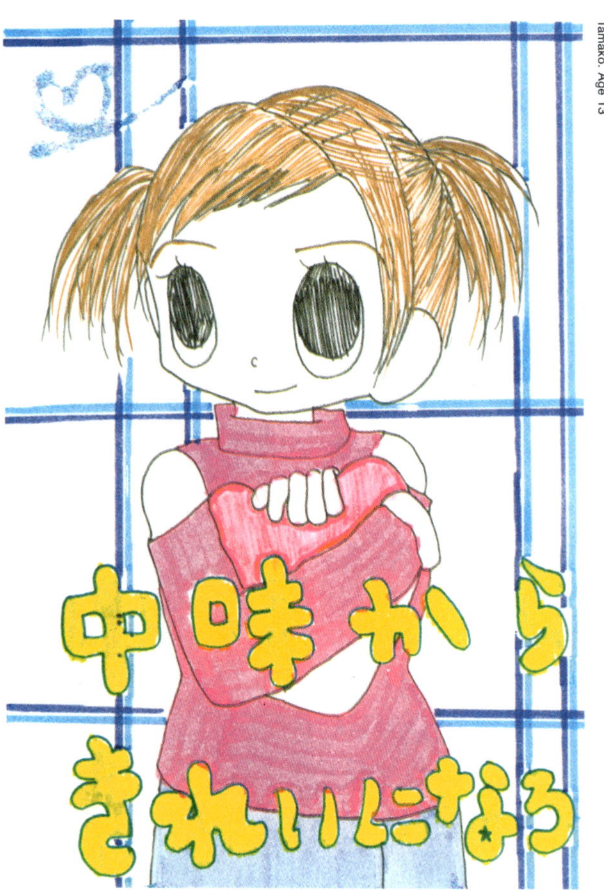

Tamako. Age 13

Be beautiful from inside.

Hanada yui. Age 13

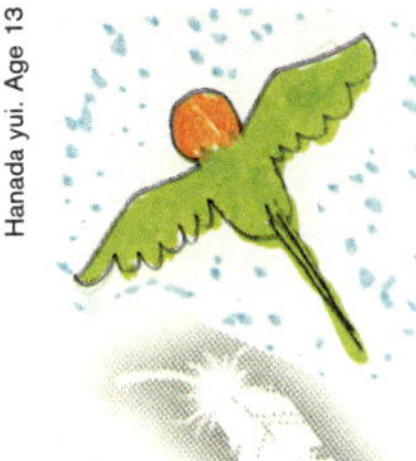

5年と10ヵ月…
いっしょにいた、わたしの
インコは、この大空に
永遠の旅にでた。

悲しいけど…いっぱい
泣いたけど、でも、もう
大丈夫だよ。

だって、思い出は
ずっと心に残ってい
るのだから…
ずっと…

今までありがとう
ピーちゃん。
ずっと忘れない。

We spent five years and ten months together…then you, my parakeet, Pi-chan, flew to the sky forever. Don't worry Pi-chan, I am fine although I have been sad and cried very much. Thank you Pi-chan, I will never forget.

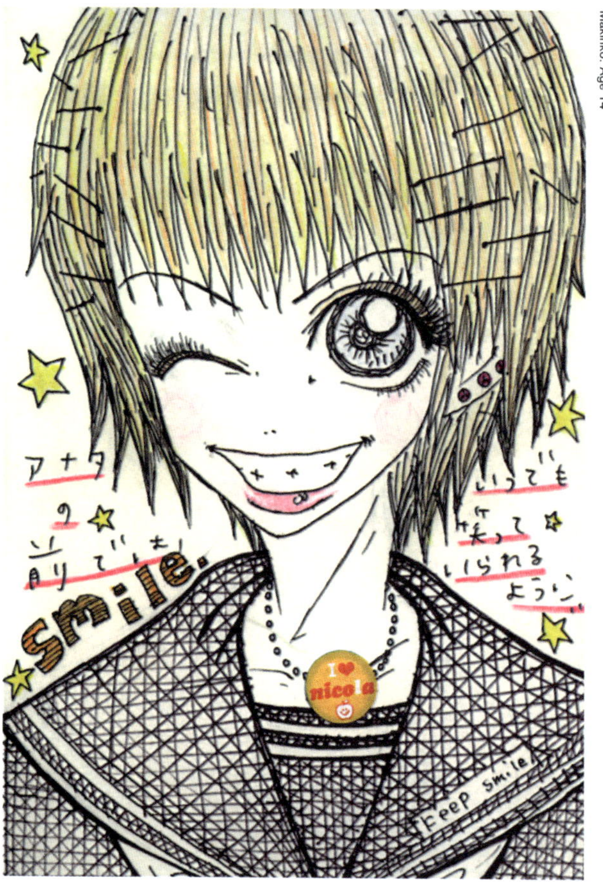

Makinko. Age 14

I try to keep smiling when I'm with you…

Nana. Age 14

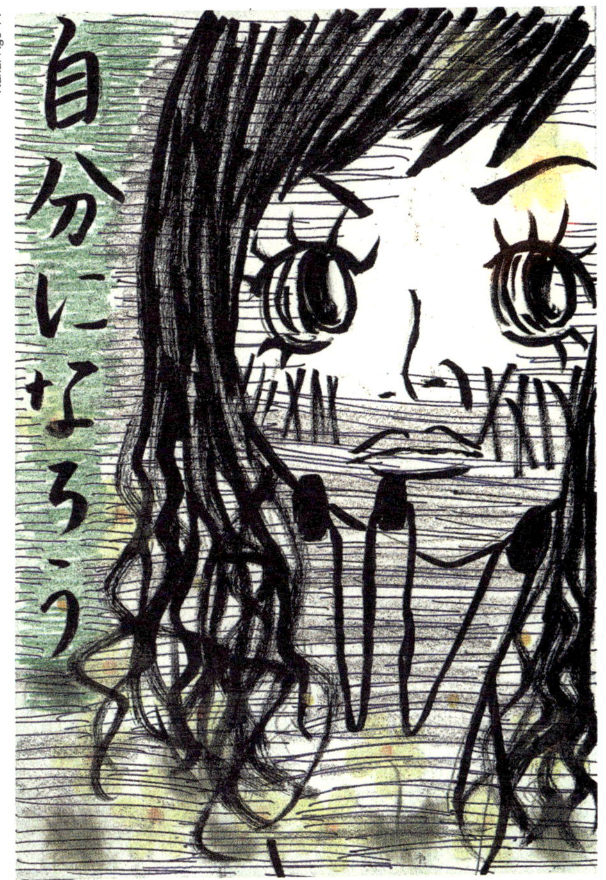

Be yourself.

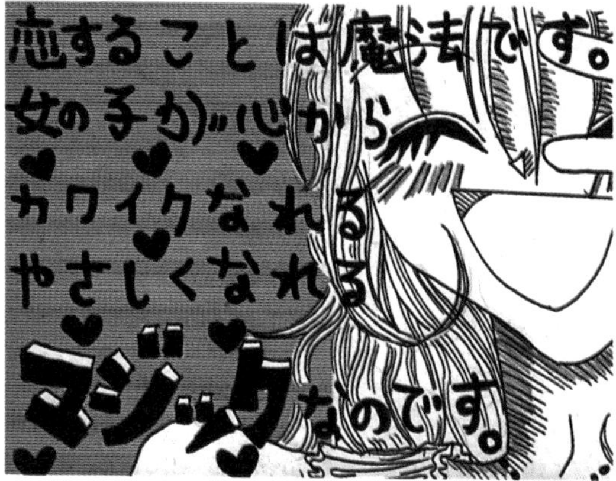

It's a magic falling love with someone. It makes girls feel warm, look pretty.

Mio. Age 12

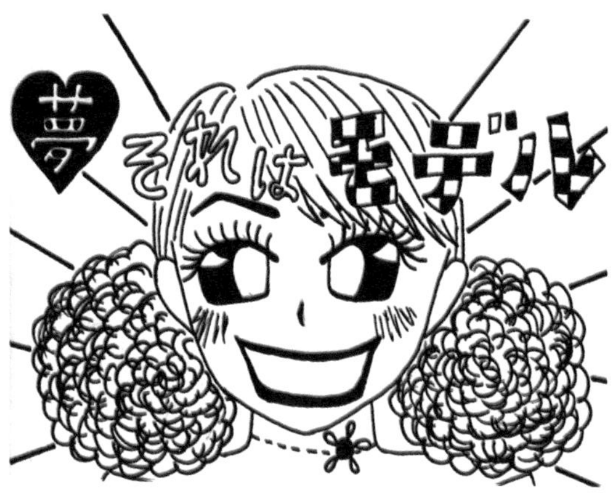

My dream, it's being a model.

Mizuho Fukushima. Age 13

Akari. Age 12

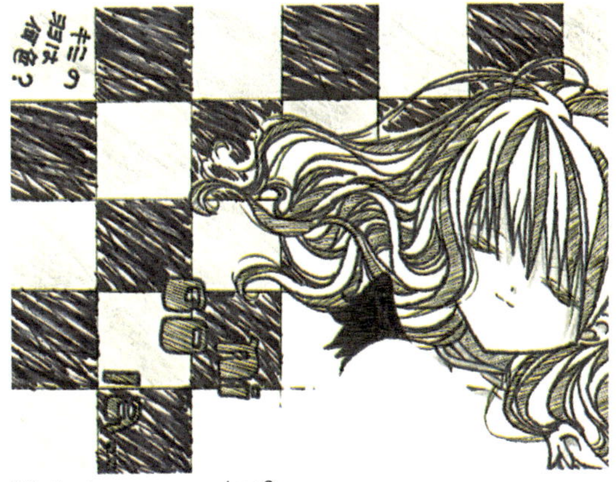

What colour are your wings?

Aya. Age 15

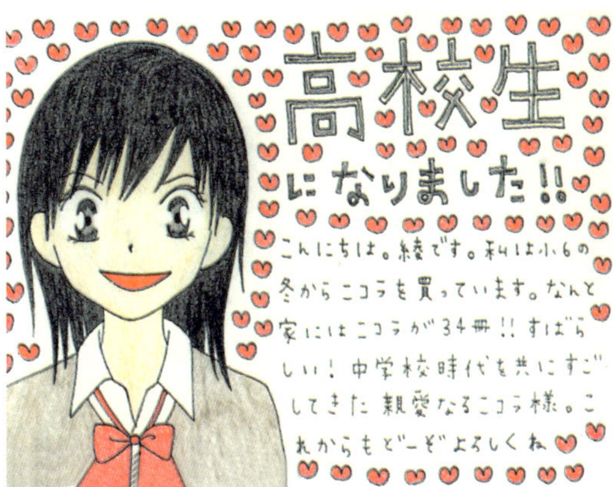

I became a high school student!! Hi, It's Aya. I've read Nicola for 3 years!! Great! I've been with you all through junior high school. Thank you!

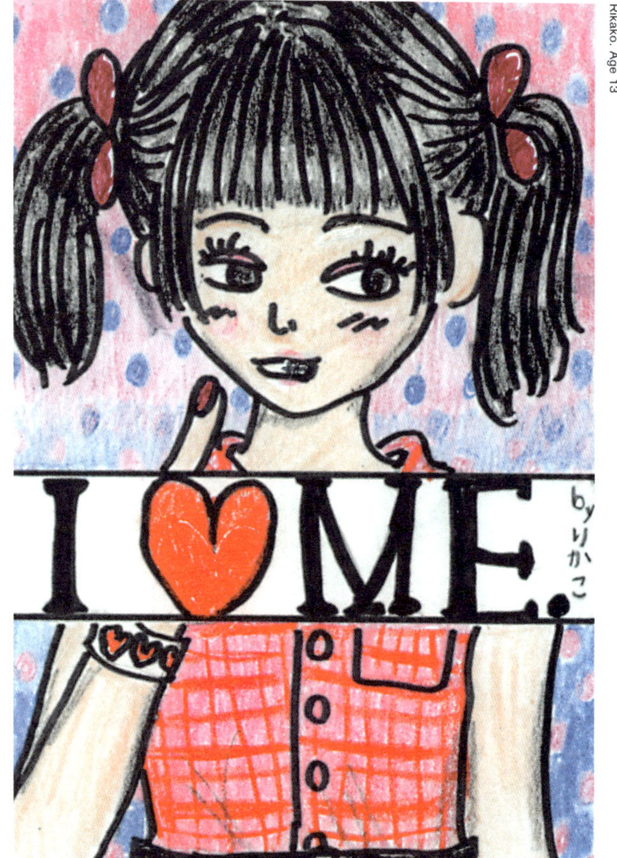

Rikako. Age 13

Cherry. Age 13

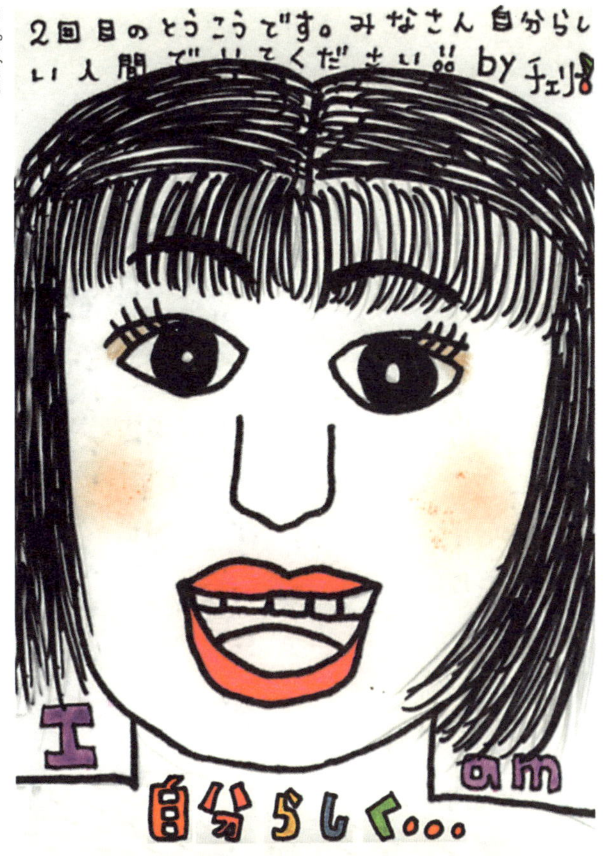

Be yourself…

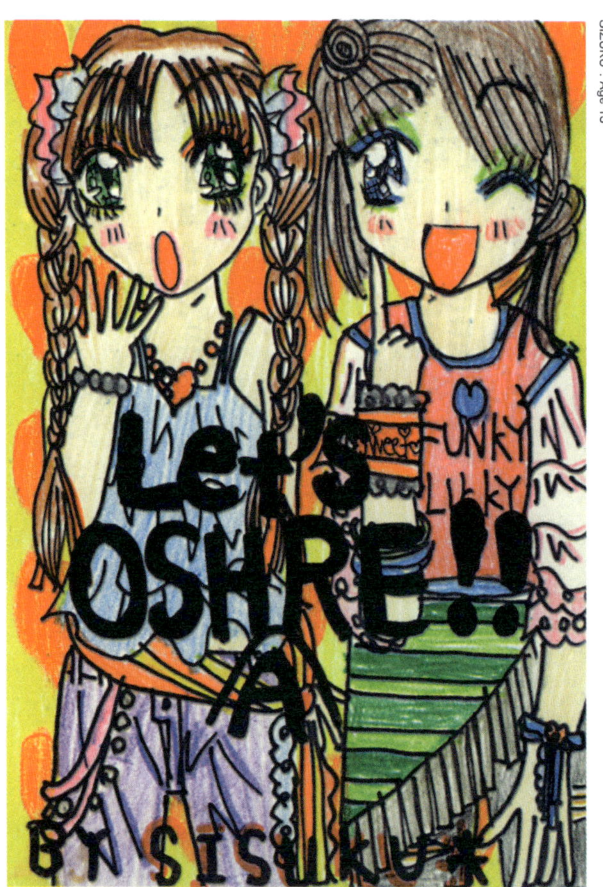

SIZUKU*, Age 13

Let's dress up!!

Momoka. Age 14

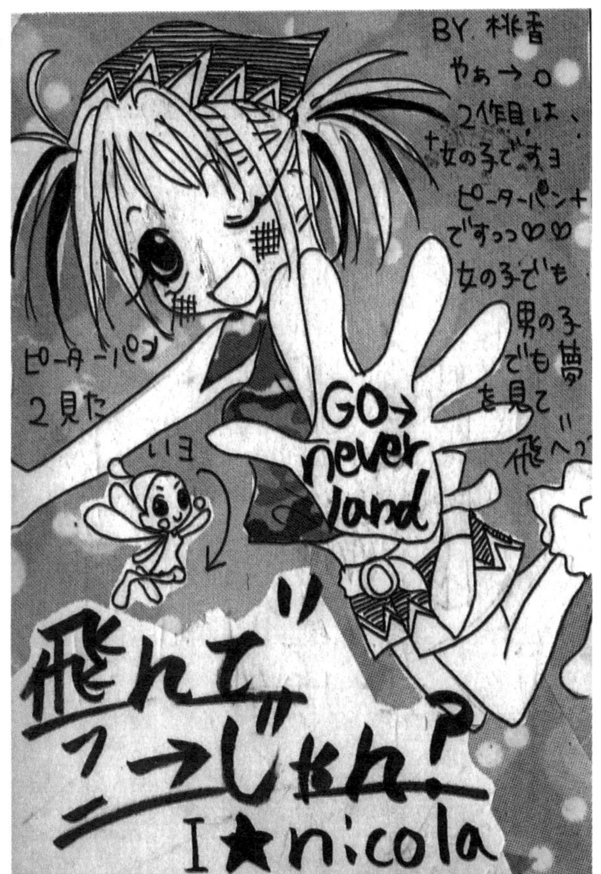

This is a Girl Peter Pan. Both boys & girls, fly toward your dreams!! Go to the never land. Let's fly, shall we?

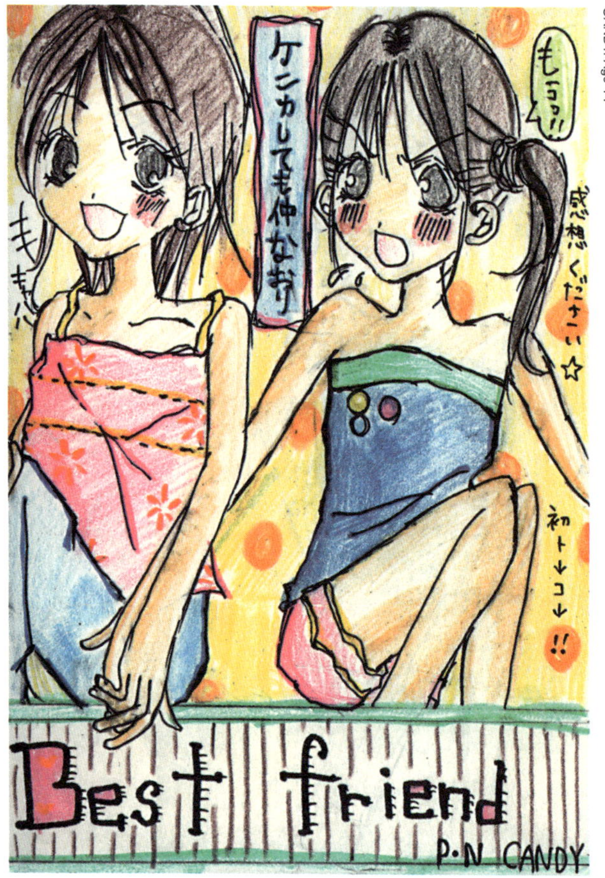

Be friends again

Honoka. Age 12

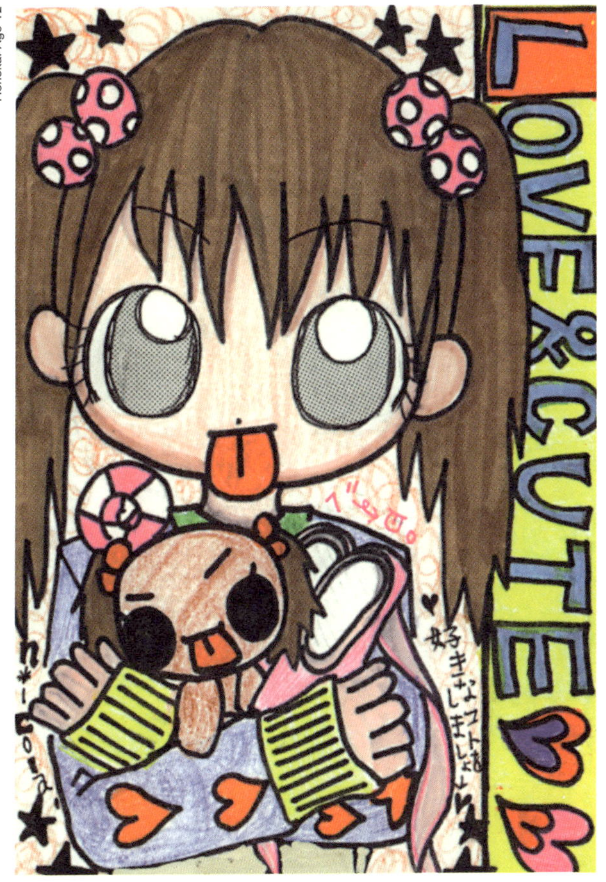

Love & Cute ; Let's do things you want to do, shall we?

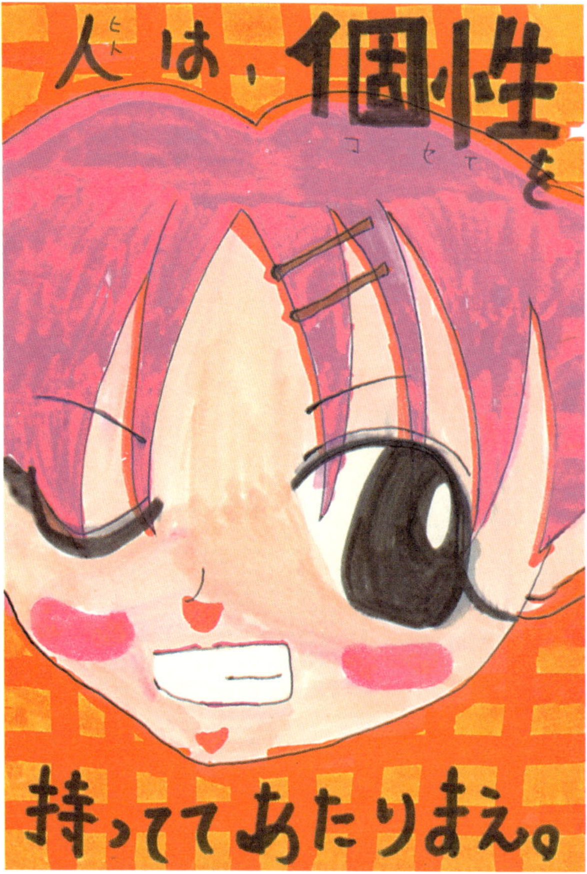

人は、個性を持っててあたりまえ。

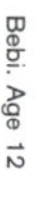

Everyone should have their individualities.

Sourei. Age 13

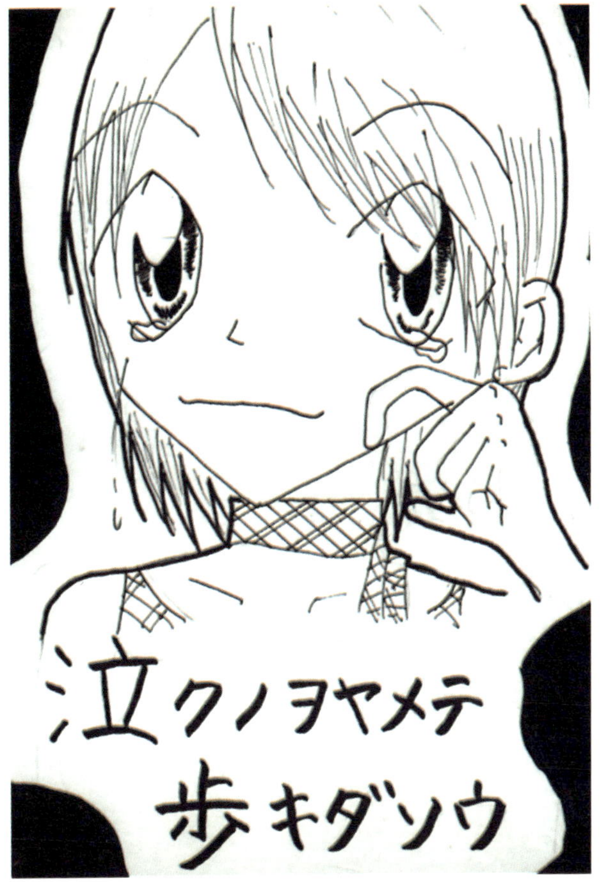

Stop crying, then start walking

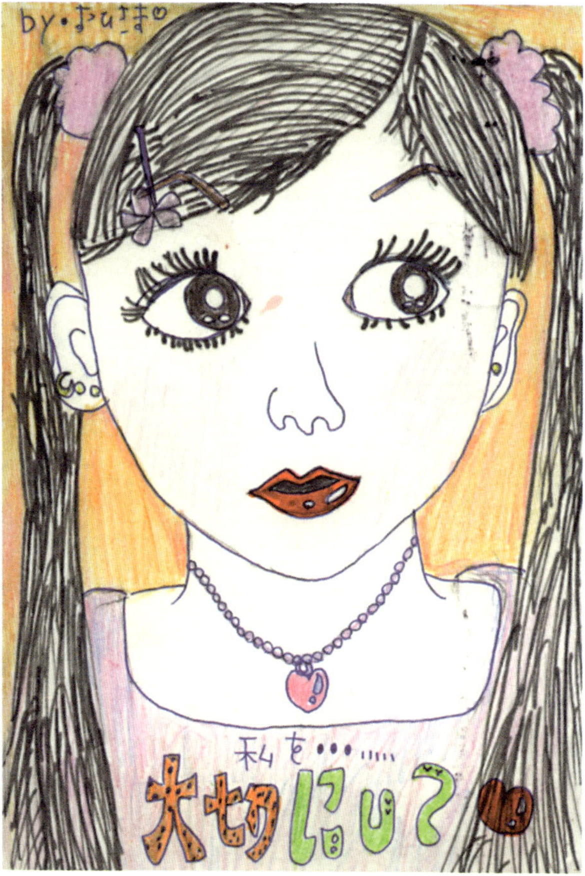

Ohisama. Age 13

Give me your care.

Age 13

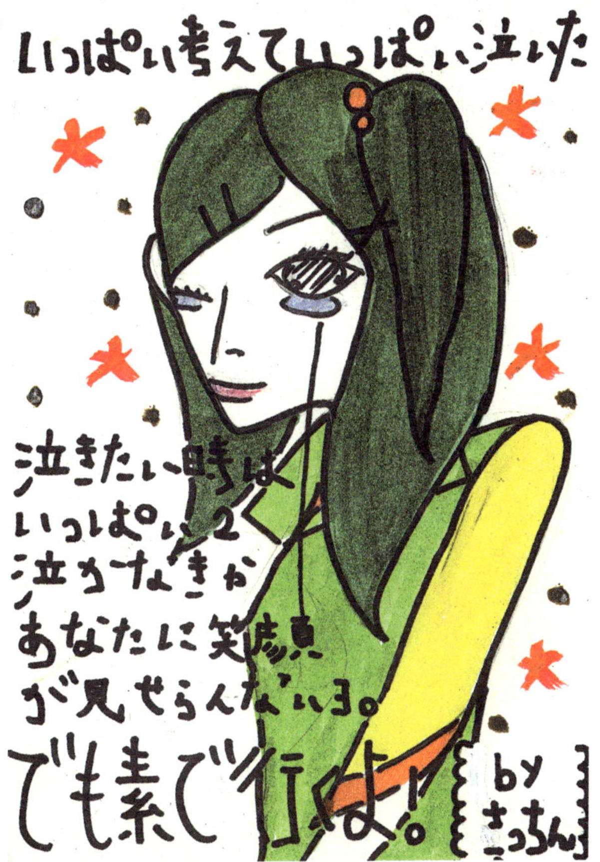

I thought a lot and cried a lot. When I feel like crying, I should cry, otherwise I can't give you a smile. Be myself!)

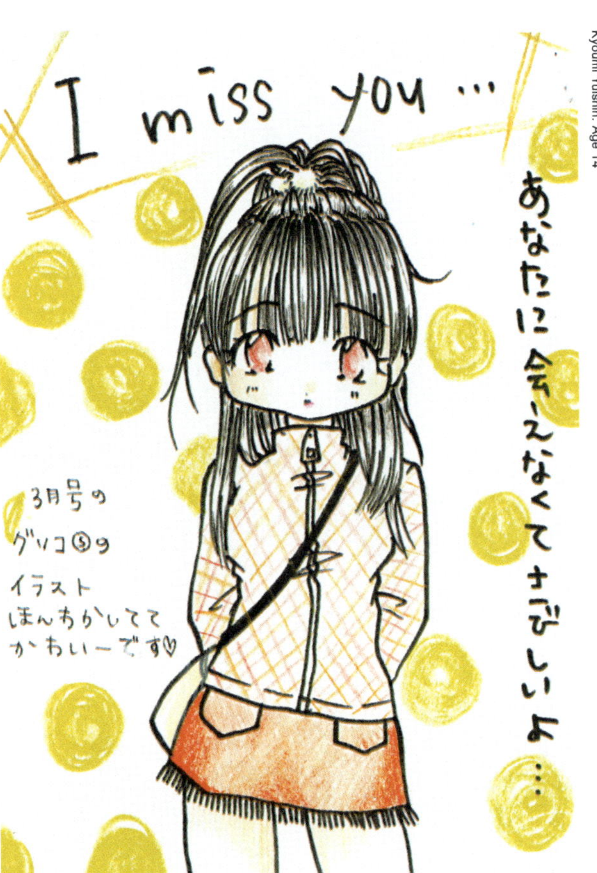

Kyoumi Yuishin. Age 14

I miss you…

Teria. Age 14

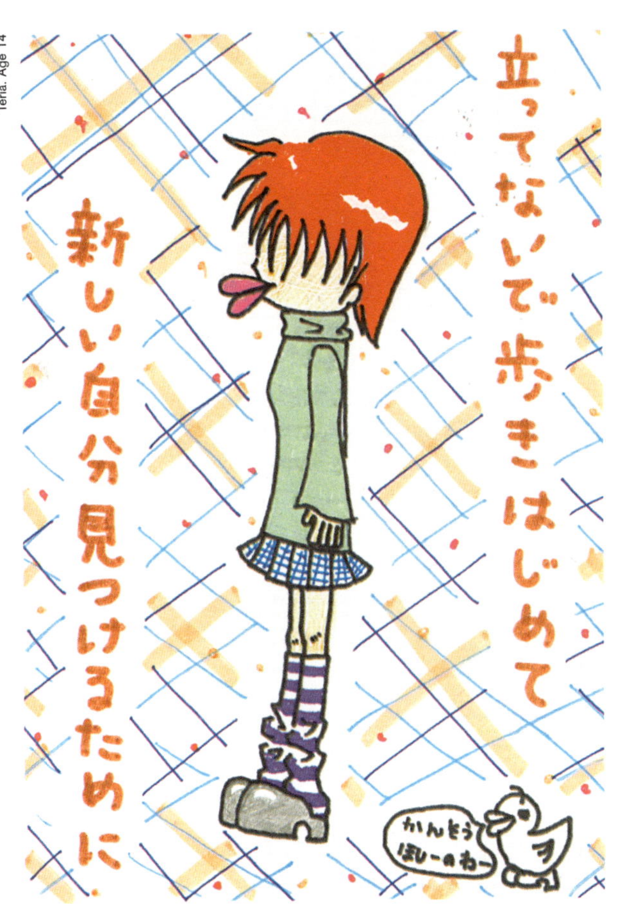

Don't just stand around, do start walking, so that you will find yourself.

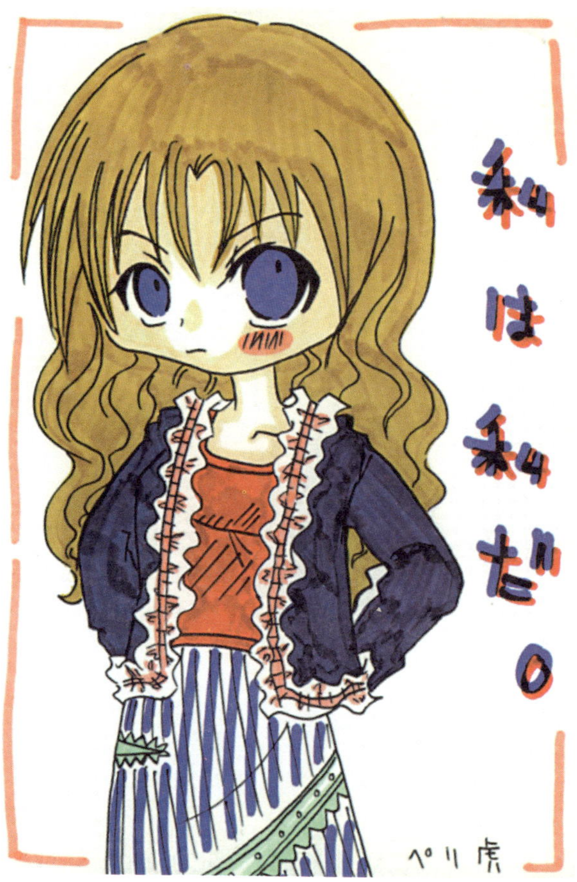

Peritora. Age 12

I am me.

KAKERA. Age 13

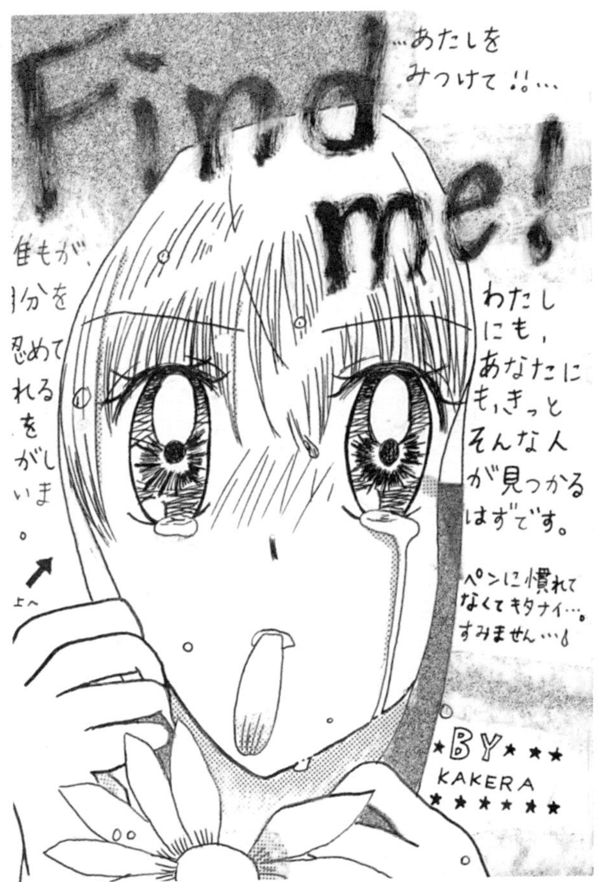

Find me! Everyone is looking for someone who accepts themselves. We can find that someone.

The Author

Editor wizard Yonehara is one of a kind. He conceives and edits countless magazines linked with Japanese street culture. His wide range of activities include his first magazine Egg, which formed the Shibuya Style of super tanned and over made-up school "gals". Out of Photographers, a magazine compiled solely of amateur photographs from all over Japan makes an authentic monthly Japanese photo-album. One of his latest projects is Smart Girls, a magazine that combines sex and fashion for both sexes.

Special thanks to: All Nicola Readers, Nicola editorial Staff, Norihisa Hirao (AMG), Chihiro Kida (Chihiro), Masaya Kinoshita (Masayo), Rie Iwamoto, Namba Family, Yohko Yonehara, and Chikako Yonehara.

I Am Me

What of the thoughts, fears, hopes and desires of children in Japan, a society that enforces the sacrifice of individual expression for the demands of the community? From the mail-bags of Nicola, a Japanese magazine for girls in their early teens, Yonehara and Pocko have edited a selection of the thousands of illustrated post-cards sent in by readers. The drawings and messages that adorn them amount to snapshots of the girl's inner worlds, encoded in the idio-matic phrasing and imagery of Japanese popular culture.

Here the familiar language is used as the means of expres-sion for nascent personalities, for individuals struggling to make themselves heard. The optimism and sweetness is undermined by an existential under-current of self-doubt, alongside the familiar anxiety of the need to be accepted.

The Pocko Collection...it keeps growing!

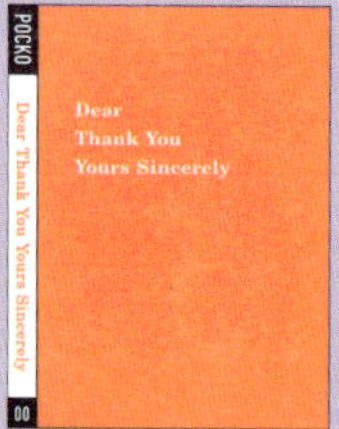

00 **Dear Thank You Yours Sincerely**
Atsuhide Ito

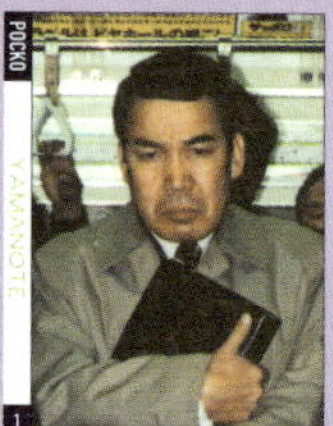

1 **Yamanote**
Iñigo Asís

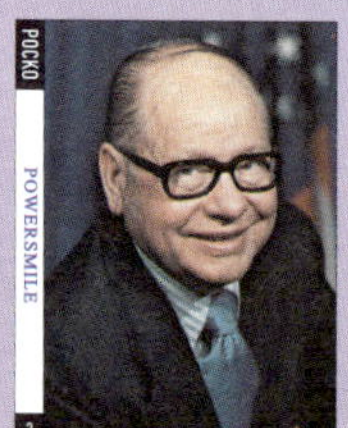

2 **Power Smile**
Adam Lowe

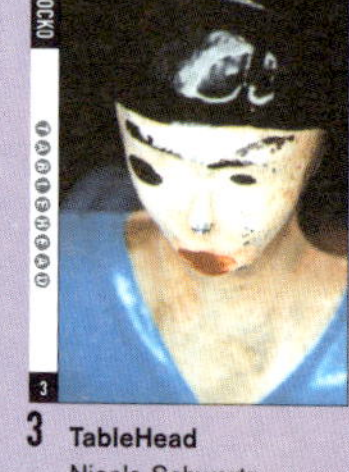

3 **TableHead**
Nicola Schwartz

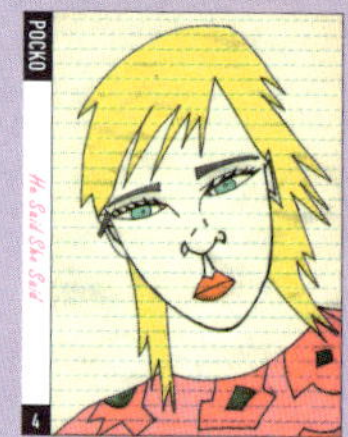

4 **He Said, She Said**
Daisy de Villeneuve

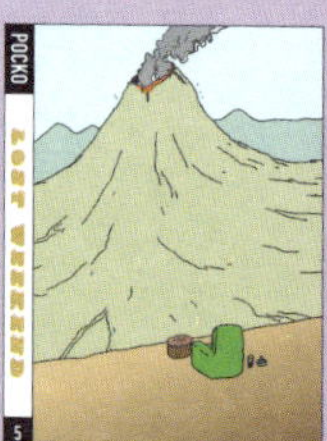

5 **Lost Weekend**
Paul McDevitt